COOKING WITH MUSHROOMS

COOKING WITH MUSHROOMS

A Fungi Lover's Guide to the
World's Most Versatile, Flavorful,
Health-Boosting Ingredients

ANDREA GENTL

ARTISAN BOOKS | NEW YORK

Library of Congress Cataloging-in-Publication Data is on file.
ISBN 978-1-64829-150-0

Design by Su Barber

Artisan books are available at special discounts when purchased
in bulk for premiums and sales promotions as well as for fund-
raising or educational use. Special editions or book excerpts
also can be created to specification. For details, contact the
Special Sales Director at the address below, or send an e-mail
to specialmarkets@workman.com. For speaking engagements,
contact speakersbureau@workman.com.

Published by Artisan
A division of Workman Publishing Co., Inc.
225 Varick Street
New York, NY 10014-4381
artisanbooks.com

Artisan is a registered trademark of Workman Publishing Co., Inc.
Printed in China on responsibly sourced paper
First printing, October 2022

10 9 8 7 6 5 4 3 2 1

As soon as I left home in my teens, I cooked. I cooked to remind myself where I came from and to bring people together. Cooking for people felt natural and became a way to share with others. Whatever the occasion, we gathered: for dinners in cramped apartments, on fire escapes, by reservoirs deep into the night, in fields upstate, and at raucous dance parties in the woods. Through our early twenties and into our thirties, after 9/11 and into our forties, through marriages, births, divorces, deaths of friends, grandparents, and parents, and through one global pandemic, we gathered. This book is dedicated to all the people—both family and chosen family—who have shared a meal, cooked together, and leaned on one another in hard times. The table kept us grounded. This book is for all of those people, but especially for my forever dining companions—Lula, Sam, and Marty, my true north.

CONTENTS

INTRODUCTION

I am a mushroom enthusiast and an avid home cook, a curious market scavenger, and a keen observer of the natural world. In my work as a photographer for the past thirty years, I've had the great privilege to travel the globe. Many of my recipe inspirations and their flavor profiles come from those travels. After a childhood spent traipsing through the wild, I rediscovered the untamed and varied world of mushrooms—the diverse, healthy, adaptogenic magic mycelia of the fungi kingdom—through photography.

I have always been a bit obsessed with mushrooms. I drew them constantly as a kid. Later in my twenties, I came to love them even more through my work. I am captivated by beauty in nature and food, and mushrooms have been my constant muse. In photographing the work of some of the world's best chefs and many of their incredible cookbooks, I gained an invaluable education, picking up something from every chef I have worked with as I peppered them with questions. I am drawn to books that tell a story, and to chefs with a strong point of view. Truthfully, I started my culinary education, like so many people, at my grandmother's knee. Through her, I possess a strong sense of ancestral taste. Anchovies, capers, garlic, olives, salty pecorino, almonds, and bitter greens are the foods in my blood.

While photographing *Baking with Julia*, some twenty-five years after dipping biscotti in my nonna's espresso, I started my culinary photographic education. Julia Child came to our loft in SoHo for lunch on one of the shoot days. She was marvelous. A few weeks later, when we went to Cambridge to shoot on location, I was struck by the simple beauty of her kitchen. Every tool had a place. Her hands reached instinctively for a whisk as she showed us the drawings that outlined each tool. The kitchen was absolutely unassuming, plain by today's somewhat ostentatious, Instagram-ready standards, really. Everything was comfortable, and I got the sense that Julia liked to cook with her hands, whisking cream, kneading bread, and mixing pastry dough (I still make the pie pastry from that book). I feel, though I can't say for certain, that she had no use for machines. I didn't see many in her kitchen. Many of the chefs I have worked with have this in common with Julia, a sense of what is tactile and what is possible to make with their own hands. I've picked up this sense from Julia and the other chefs and try to use my hands whenever possible in the kitchen. I find cooking by hand to be meditative and prefer a whisk to an electric beater any day.

Years after working on *Baking with Julia*, I traveled to northern Sweden, where I experienced one of the best meals I have ever eaten, at Fäviken. I spent three days at the restaurant trailing its chef, Magnus Nilsson, in the kitchen, the garden, and the woods. His food was deeply delicious, wildly creative, hyperlocal, slightly uncomfortable, and completely sustainable. He cooked with the foods that surrounded him from the field, forest, and mountain. The pine, spruce, mushrooms, and moss—all of it was new to me in the culinary realm but wildly familiar to me visually and in an olfactory sense. Many of the ingredients reminded me of western Massachusetts, where I grew up. My family's very small farm was surrounded by ancient oaks, sugar maples, and soft willowy pines, and was the perfect environment for mushrooms to grow. I spent the better part of my childhood outside, roaming the woods and fields around our home, my pockets filled with bits of sticks, wood, moss, hay, mushrooms, acorns, and pinecones. I was attracted to many of these things because of how they smelled, and those smells still have the most intense links to memory for me.

I attribute my strong connection with nature to all the time I spent exploring the woods in those days, identifying plants and discovering wild foods. The more time you spend in nature, the more you notice the cycle of seasons, and the more you connect. In my neighborhood, almost everyone's mother was an herbalist. Talk of plants surrounded us constantly. At Fäviken, I experienced a "remembering." My whole world changed after that trip. I came home and immediately started making finishing salts with pine and spruce, and fermenting flowers. I began making butter, the memory of which was embedded in my youth, having grown up with two Jersey cows that provided us with enough thick yellow cream to make the most delicious butter and clotted cream for shortcakes.

When I moved to New York City for school, I left the woods, the farm girl, and the smell of hay and wet leaves behind (though hay and wet leaves are still two of my favorite smells!). After Fäviken, I realized my somewhat hippie upbringing was right here with me the whole time. Once these olfactory memories were triggered, I started to understand food in the "time and place" realm, and began my blog, *Hungry Ghost Food and Travel*, shortly thereafter. The blog served as an exploration of wild and gathered foods from around the globe, travel stories, personal essays, recipes, and tributes to my ancestors.

As a photographer, travel for work has influenced the way I eat and cook more than anything else. Wherever I go, I explore local markets and look for ingredients to squirrel away in my bag and bring home to incorporate into my cooking. I talk to people I meet along the way about food, foraging,

and native ingredients. I usually come away with new knowledge and inspiration. At home, I'm a regular at my local farmers' market year-round. I usually go to the market without any idea of what I am going to make, letting the ingredients inspire me. These days the most inspiring ingredient is the mysterious and magical mushroom!

In the past few years, there has been a notable shift in cultivated mushroom availability. Gone are the days of supermarket button mushrooms under plastic wrap as the sole option for the curious home cook. Specialty mushrooms once available only to foragers and chefs are now widely sold in nearly every size, shape, and color. Farmers' markets are teeming with piles of puffy lion's manes, maitakes, and oyster mushrooms (in yellow, blue, gray, and pink), and many grocers stock multiple varieties beyond the ubiquitous white buttons. The wellness boom has catapulted dried mushrooms like chaga and reishi into the adaptogenic stratosphere, lending their signature scents and flavors to everything from our morning tea to our evening cocktails.

As for eating mushrooms, my relationship with edible fungi has been gradual. For the first twenty-odd years of my life, the only mushrooms I encountered at the dinner table were cremini, pickled and served on my grandmother's antipasto plate, or sautéed as a component of beef Bourguignon, made famous by Julia Child's black-and-white television show, one of the only programs I was allowed to watch. Julia had an infectious enthusiasm for mushrooms. Then there were my grandmother's holiday mushrooms—again, cremini stuffed with sautéed stems, bread crumbs, parsley, copious amounts of garlic, white wine, and pecorino. Those mushrooms became the inspiration for my Thanksgiving stuffing; it's essentially the same flavor profile, just with a larger proportion of sourdough bread.

In my late twenties, while on assignment in northern California, I met and photographed Connie Green, the famous wildcrafter and supplier of wild mushrooms to Bay Area chefs. We trailed her one morning through the woods near Sea Ranch, as she collected an enormous variety of edible mushrooms. I had never seen such a basket of diversity. I can't remember if she found any candy cap mushrooms that morning, but I recall her telling me that they had a sweetness that smelled of maple syrup, perfect for desserts. After our woods walk, we ate piles of mushrooms sautéed in butter and shaved raw mushrooms with salty butter on crusty toasted bread.

Years later, I struck up a friendship with some wildcrafters I met at the New Amsterdam Market in Lower Manhattan. Nova Kim and Les Hook, Vermonters with over eighty years of wild food gathering experience between them, frequented the Sunday market. The first time I came upon their stall, I was mesmerized by the hen of the woods (also known as maitake), bearded tooth (also known as lion's mane), chicken of the woods, and matsutake mushrooms, each fresh from the earth, bits of sticks and leaves still stuck to their stems. The mushrooms they offered struck a familiar chord, and I suddenly realized I had seen them throughout my whole childhood in the woods around my home. Nova gave me all kinds of helpful advice on how to cook them. I started coming back every week, and she and Les would reach below their table to pull out a box of the most beautiful mushrooms they had saved for me. I started cooking with them—dehydrating some, making stocks with others, weaving mushrooms into my everyday cooking. I was lucky enough to spend some extended time with them, at which point I relearned how to see the woods and the incredible bounty it offers. I was reminded of the beautiful cycle of life and death in nature that mimics our own. Today, thanks to the enormous growing interest in mushrooms, I can find many of the varieties they introduced to me at farmers' markets, specialty shops, and grocery stores.

Mushrooms are widely hailed as the new superfood; they have many health benefits, and their texture and flavors are rich enough to substitute for meat in many dishes, and to accompany meat, poultry, fish, and eggs in many others. Dried and powdered, they take on a rich umami flavor and depth.

We are now in on the secret that most of the world has known forever: Once you start cooking with mushrooms, you will never stop. Throughout the pages of this book, I share my favorite ways to use mushrooms in drinks, broths, soups and stews, bread, breakfast dishes, salads, and sandwiches, and twists on classic dishes such as risotto and lasagna. I hope you find these recipes intriguing, and are as captivated by the mushrooms themselves—with their infinite variations in shape, texture, color, and aroma—as I have been since childhood, and continue to be.

1

THE MUSHROOMS

In this book, I am focusing on nearly two dozen of the more accessible, cultivated varieties as well as a few wild mushrooms. Most of the mushrooms can be found at your local farmers' market or grocer. You can, of course, substitute your wild finds (once properly identified, of course) into many of these recipes, but remember that not all mushrooms taste the same. Some are mild, others are briny, and some have strong, earthy flavors. Get to know your mushrooms before choosing to swap one in for another. The beautiful maple taste and smell of candy caps, for example, works best in desserts, so they are not a good substitute for other mushrooms in savory dishes.

Mushrooms are an incredibly versatile ingredient. They are beautiful, flavorful, and mysterious, and can be humble or elevated. A simple dish of mushrooms sautéed in butter is one of the most flavorful things you can eat. Mushrooms can be free when found in nature, sometimes inexpensive depending on the variety, or worth their weight in gold. Mushrooms around the world are anticipated as a sign of the changing seasons; a giant plate is cause for celebration. They are elusive, and do as they wish, popping up one year here and the next year there. They grow in forests and fields and on trees alive and dead. They appear in recently disturbed earth after logging and forest fires. Mushrooms come in all shapes and sizes, with varieties that hide in broad daylight, and others that glow in the dark. Mushrooms can range from a dark inky indigo to white, black, brown, gray, orange, and all colors in between. Mushrooms communicate with each other, and some varieties can camouflage themselves to hide from predators.

Notably, mushrooms are not plants. It is said they are more human than the plant world, but they exist in a kingdom by themselves, the wild and magical kingdom of fungi. We know that all mushrooms are not edible, but how did we get to this point of knowing? I imagine, though I can't know, it was through trial and error or perhaps some innate sense that early humans had with regard to what to pick and what not to pick; perhaps they watched carefully to see what animals ate. I have great respect for mushrooms. I only eat what I am absolutely certain is edible.

Indigenous peoples have a long-standing relationship with mushrooms, specifically with culinary usage and ceremonial purposes. Many of the world's ancient cultures have been wise to the merits of eating fungi for thousands of years. Generally speaking, mushrooms are considered to be healthy. They are often adaptogenic and high in protein and minerals, as well as B and D vitamins.

MUSHROOM TERMINOLOGY

ADAPTOGEN: An adaptogen is any substance from nature—usually roots, herbs, or fungi—that can aid the body's response to external stressors. Many mushrooms are considered adaptogenic, including chaga, cordyceps, reishi, lion's mane, and shiitake (see Note on page 58).

FUNGI: The biological kingdom made up of any number of spore-producing organisms that feed and grow on organic matter; this includes mold, mildew, mushrooms, and yeast.

FUNGICULTURE: The cultivation of mushrooms and other fungi.

INOCULATE: To introduce a mushroom spawn into a growing medium. In the natural world, this is often a log or stump; indoors, inoculation occurs on a material known as substrate.

MYCELIUM: The vegetative body of fungi, which includes a vast network of very fine, thin strands known as hyphae.

MYCOLOGY: The study of the fungi kingdom, which includes mushrooms, mold, mildew, and yeast.

SPAWN: In the cultivation of mushrooms, spawn is used in much the same way as seeds are used to grow vegetables. This is the mycelium itself that's grown indefinitely on a substrate.

SPORES: Spores are what mushrooms release in the reproductive process; the best way to identify mushrooms in the wild is to do a spore print, letting the spores fall onto a piece of paper placed just beneath the cap for several hours until a pattern and color of the spores are presented. Every mushroom has a unique configuration, by which the mushroom can be identified.

SUBSTRATE: The material on which to grow cultivated mushrooms is called substrate; in the wild, that includes rotting logs and other organic materials. For cultivation purposes, substrate can be cardboard, sawdust, or grains such as rye, wheat, or millet.

A Note on Gathering Wild Mushrooms

The mushroom kingdom boasts more than a hundred thousand known varieties, and countless unknown ones, too. Many are prized for their distinct flavors, textures, shapes, sizes, and colors, and are sought after for healthful and medicinal purposes. In many parts of the world, gathering mushrooms is as much a routine as ritual. The hunt for mushrooms is an adventure, but admittedly one that's best left to those with the experience and know-how to avoid picking anything questionable. "Look-alike" varieties resemble common varieties but are not safe to eat, and many wild mushrooms contain toxins that can cause illness or, in extreme cases, death. In this book, I recommend some commonly cultivated mushrooms that can also be found in the wild. However, this is not a wild mushroom book. If you choose to collect mushrooms, you must learn how to identify them.

Mushrooms can only be identified by doing a proper spore print. If you would like to learn more about collecting wild mushrooms, there are some great publications in Recommended Reading (page 233).

NOTES ON FRESH MUSHROOMS

On Shopping for Fresh Mushrooms

For the freshest and widest variety of mushrooms, I highly recommend getting to know the mushroom vendors at your local market. Ask lots of questions; vendors are most often happy to share their knowledge with fellow mushroom lovers. You can learn a lot about how to prepare and cook mushrooms, and what to look for in the market at what times of year, by talking to the sellers.

When shopping for fresh mushrooms, use all your senses to determine freshness. Touch them if possible; mushrooms should feel heavy in the hand, alive, plump, and firm. Avoid anything with soft, damp, or slimy spots, or mushrooms that feel dried out or wrinkled. Notice their colors, which should appear uniform throughout the cap; steer clear of discoloration. Sniff the mushrooms, to make sure the smell is earthy. They can sometimes smell funky, which does not always mean they are rotten. (Avoid mushrooms that smell like ammonia, a sure sign that they have turned.) Look to see that the caps are tightly closed and the gills (if the mushroom has them) appear fresh (gills are a sign that the mushroom has reached peak maturity). Try to buy mushrooms of the same size within each variety, so that they'll cook evenly (you can always chop or tear large ones as needed before cooking, however).

Cultivated mushrooms are pretty widely available at supermarkets and groceries; look for organic options whenever possible. The most common varieties, often wrapped in plastic, include button, cremini, portobello, and shiitake. I would avoid buying any pre-cut mushrooms or anything wrapped in plastic, which suffocates the mushrooms. There really is no good way to tell how long they have been wrapped up. Instead, look for supermarkets or grocery stores that have open bins of mushrooms. Choosing your own is always a better option. Specialty grocers and Asian markets are likely to have a wider selection of other varieties, especially maitake, oyster, beech, wood ear, and enoki. You will sometimes find these wrapped in plastic; if that is the only way to buy them, check to ensure that they are firm and fresh with a pleasant aroma.

On Pricing

As you explore the world of edible mushrooms, you will soon realize that prices can vary greatly. Some varieties are infinitely more expensive than others. If you find that one variety is prohibitive for a certain recipe, please explore another variety. I have given suggestions for swaps whenever possible. Another option is to buy a smaller quantity and fill in the remainder with a more affordable type. This way, you'll get a chance to experience the difference in flavors and textures of each mushroom. Mushrooms are incredibly versatile, and experimentation by way of swapping varieties is always encouraged.

On Dirt

For the most part, when buying fresh cultivated mushrooms, you won't have to worry much about removing dirt. Mushrooms from wildcrafters are a different story. They may have a bit of dirt on them from the woods or fields, but they are not "dirty."

Washing mushrooms is a very polarizing topic. Because mushrooms are like sponges and absorb any moisture they come in contact with, they should be cleaned just before cooking. I like to clean wild mushrooms with a small paintbrush that I keep in my kitchen. (A dedicated soft toothbrush works fine as well.) I stick to the hard-and-fast rule of never washing mushrooms, whether they are cultivated or wild.

Some people feel fine about giving mushrooms a quick rinse. If you must do so, you can gently but quickly plunge them into a bowl of lukewarm water and swoosh them around, then set them on a clean, dry tea towel. Blot them dry right away, to remove any remaining water. The key is not to soak them, lest they take on water and turn mushy or slimy.

Once they have been brushed or plunged, trim the mushrooms of any woody ends and give them a good brushing to remove any remaining dirt, leaves, sticks, or debris, and, of course, any insects! (Humans are not the only ones who enjoy a nice mushroom meal.) If you find that the mushrooms still seem dirty, give them a gentle wipe with a clean, just-damp tea towel. Cultivated mushrooms are generally quite clean. Trim any old or woody stems and cut away any remaining

substrate (the material in which the mushroom was grown).

On Prepping

The prep work really depends on the mushroom variety and the dish that you're making, but generally, you'll want to trim off any woody ends or hard stems. Maitakes and lion's mane are gently torn and shredded by hand rather than sliced; they tear naturally along the fiber of the mushroom. Large mushrooms are often halved or quartered. Any especially woody stems, like those on chestnut and shiitake mushrooms, should be trimmed away and saved for stock. You can throw them in a quart (1 L) jar in your freezer and just keep adding to it until you have enough to make a stock or you can add them to a chicken or vegetable stock for more flavor. Some recipes call for only the caps, even if the stems are edible; you can save those stems for stock, too.

On Storing

I learned about keeping mushrooms in paper bags sorted by variety from Les and Nova of Vermont Wildcrafters. Mushrooms are super happy in paper bags and terribly unhappy when stored in suffocating plastic, which causes them to become slimy and quickly rot.

Keep the bags open or very loosely closed at the top, and store them in the refrigerator for no more than a couple of days. If you must buy mushrooms in plastic-wrapped containers, replace the plastic with paper as soon as you get home.

GROWING YOUR OWN MUSHROOMS

If you're curious about mushroom varieties that you can't find at your local grocers or farmers' markets, try a mushroom growing kit. In the past few years, growing mushrooms in yards and community gardens, in raised beds, or even in mulch piles and other warm spots has become super popular. My Instagram feed is populated with many small mushroom growers; during the early days of the pandemic, the popularity of grow kits hit a feverish spike.

I love mushroom kits and have cultivated many types of oyster mushrooms (pictured left), cordyceps, and lion's mane successfully in my kitchen. During our lockdown time in upstate New York, I had several varieties growing in big blocks all down my staircase. Growing mushrooms is like having magic at your fingertips. The blocks seem inactive at first and then suddenly they flush and grow right before your eyes. They can double in size in a day. Keep an eye on them if it is especially humid, as they can become heavy with moisture and rot quickly.

Mushroom kits are an easy way to familiarize yourself with different varieties of mushrooms, to learn about how they grow, and to see if you might want to grow them on a larger scale. If you do, there is a plethora of information available in books and videos and online, and, of course, you can always chat with mushroom farmers.

Designed to grow on kitchen counters or outside, the kits are made of substrate blocks (consisting of cardboard, natural wood shavings or dust, grains, or some combination of materials) implanted with the mycelium, or spawn. The blocks are wrapped in plastic. After unpacking the kit and cutting open the plastic, you mist it with water regularly. The mycelium responds immediately to oxygen and humidity, spurring growth. Over the course of just a few weeks, depending on the type and kit maker, the mushrooms should be ready to harvest and cook. You should be able to get two or three flushes (crops) from one kit, and maybe a few more afterward. After the last flush, take the kit outside and leave it in your garden or under some ferns. It will likely keep sprouting mushrooms, though it can be a matter of months rather than weeks for them to colonize and fruit.

Many people place the blocks in the compost, where they will continually sprout once they colonize.

There's an abundance of places to buy the kits these days, locally and online. Oysters in blue, pink, and golden hues are a nice option for those new to mushroom growing, and those who live in varying climates. They're considered fail-proof. Some are so vigorous that they may even start growing before you open the box and the plastic wrapping. Lion's mane kits are also great for beginners, and they are so otherworldly in appearance and divine in taste. Shiitakes are best grown on logs, as in nature; the process takes longer than growing mushrooms from kits indoors, perhaps even a year or more. They will seem completely inactive and then suddenly flush with pounds of shiitakes.

COOKING MUSHROOMS

Generally speaking, mushrooms are best eaten cooked, even briefly. All mushrooms cook best at high heat, with lots of fat (I generally cook them in butter, olive oil, or ghee). The heat helps rid the mushrooms of excess water as it concentrates their flavor. Mushrooms release their own liquid as they cook, then absorb the fat to make up for that lost moisture, becoming intense flavor bombs in the process.

Take care not to crowd the pan when cooking mushrooms. You want to give them room to cook on their own and release water, so they sear rather than steam (it's the mushy squeakiness that you're avoiding). For the best flavor and texture, brown them just until you can smell the mushrooms. Avoid salting mushrooms too early, as it will draw out moisture and turn them rubbery instead of nicely seared and caramelized.

SAUTÉ: Sautéing is one of the easiest and most familiar methods for cooking mushrooms. Start by heating up butter, olive oil, or ghee in a skillet, then add whole, sliced, or torn mushrooms. Cook by tossing the mushrooms until they are fragrant and just beginning to turn brown, and then add garlic and any other aromatics, stirring to incorporate them. Continue to cook until the mushrooms are browned.

DRY SAUTÉ: This method for cooking mushrooms is less well known, but it shouldn't be. To dry sauté means to cook in a hot skillet without adding any fat or other ingredients. Heat the skillet over medium-high until it is quite hot, then add chopped, torn, sliced, or whole mushrooms in a single layer. As the mushrooms start to release water, their flavors become more intense, concentrated, and "mushroomy" than when cooked with fats and aromatics. You can flavor them after dry sautéing with fats such as butter or olive oil, sauces like soy, or sweeteners like maple syrup. I use the dry sauté method to cook the mushrooms for the relish in the grilled cheese sandwiches on page 143.

ROAST: Roasting is one of my favorite ways to cook mushrooms, as it is very hands off. Roasting concentrates the flavor of mushrooms. I generally roast mushrooms in a sheet pan or a large cast-iron skillet. I add some fat, either olive oil, ghee, or butter, and a few seasonings, depending on the flavor profile I'm after.

SEAR: Searing mushrooms is a great way to get a crispy texture and golden-brown color. The key is to cook them in a skillet over medium-high heat and in a single layer, leaving them undisturbed and flipping halfway through. This usually takes about 3 minutes on each side, depending on the type and size of mushroom. Make sure to coat the pan with enough butter or oil, to keep the mushrooms from sticking as they develop a nice crust. Be sure to salt at the end, so you don't draw water out of the mushrooms too early.

GRILL: Mushrooms are delicious grilled over a flame, where they can take on a little smoky flavor. I start by oiling the grill or grill pan and getting it quite hot. Then I brush the mushrooms with a little olive oil, melted butter, or ghee, and place them over the flame or in the hot grill pan. The mushrooms will sputter a bit as they release moisture and take on a nice char.

SAUTÉ

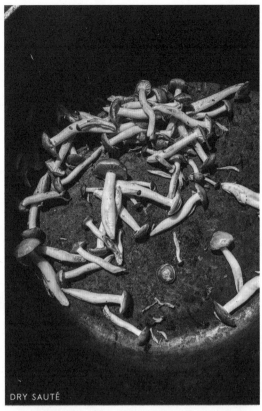

DRY SAUTÉ

SEAR

ROAST

THE MUSHROOMS

COOKING WITH MUSHROOMS

MUSHROOM VARIETIES

This book is dedicated to a mere handful of the thousands of mushroom varieties that exist. What follows is a list of the mushrooms I use most in my cooking and for the fresh and dried powders and pastes that make up my larder. It is not an exhaustive list, just the mushrooms that I rely on most for their distinct flavors, textures, and immune-boosting qualities. Most can be found at specialty grocers and farmers' markets year-round. The recipes and flavor profiles can be applied to many more varieties than I have covered here; this is meant to be a small exploration into the vast world of fungi. As a visual person, photographer, and cook, I am drawn to the beauty of the more aesthetic varieties, like maitake, oyster, lion's mane, enoki, reishi, and shiitake, which all happen to have some of the best flavors. Truth be told, however, these varieties barely hold a candle to the incredibly wide variety of wild mushrooms, which include inky blue caps, vibrant orange lobsters, and mushrooms that look like delicate branches of coral plucked from the depths of the sea, to name just a few of my many favorites. The world of wild mushrooms is something to be studied and revered, respected, and approached with caution until you can call yourself an expert.

BEECH

Beech

Beech mushrooms are named for the tree on which they commonly grow in clusters. The small, slender mushrooms are widely available in white and brown varieties. Brown beech mushrooms are the color of field mice, while the white ones resemble a chalky lime wash. Beech mushrooms are mild in flavor, a little sweet, slightly earthy, and nutty when cooked. They are a great candidate for pickling because they retain some crunch. They originated in Asia and are now cultivated in many parts of the world and sold fresh at many supermarkets, specialty grocers, and online. White beech are often packaged and labeled "Bunapi," a trademark name for a patented variety from the Hokuto Corporation. They are commonly used in soups, stews, and stir-fries, and take well to roasting and sautéing.

Candy Cap

Candy cap mushrooms are small and delicate, with a sweetly aromatic, maple-forward flavor profile and deep maple color. They are often used to flavor desserts and drinks, but in their dried form, they're used in savory dishes as well. Their smell is not as strong when fresh, but drying them releases their distinctly sweet, powerful fragrance, with notes of brown sugar and jaggery. Growing primarily along the West Coast in California and Oregon, candy caps grow in patches of moss, as well as in rotting matter and on hardwoods.

Chaga

Also known as cinder conk or black mass, chaga look nothing like mushrooms. They are dense, woody fungi that grow on birch trees, in dark, inky patches that stick out from the surface of the tree. They look almost charred, as though they have survived a fire—brown to black in color, dark on the outside and lighter reddish brown on the inside. Unlike many other mushrooms, chaga cannot be consumed in their natural state; they must be cut off from a tree with a saw and then cut or hammered into smaller pieces, which are ground into fine powder either with a very powerful processor or in a mortar and pestle. Chaga powder has an earthy, mildly sweet flavor that reminds me of maple sap, with notes of vanilla, and is widely used for teas and tinctures. It has become popular as a coffee substitute; its flavor is much smoother and less bitter than other coffee substitutes like chicory or burdock root. Medicinally, chaga has powerful anti-inflammatory properties; it also aids in lowering blood pressure and cholesterol.

Chanterelle

Chanterelle is the common name for several different species of fungi, which includes the yellow foot. One of the more well-known wild mushrooms, chanterelles are also known as girolles, and are beloved by chefs. They range in color from vibrant newt orange to butter yellow; variations in color can be found in the same patch. Chanterelles are generally 1½ to 2 inches (4 to 5 cm) in height, with a cap spread of a similar size. I have seen them much larger as well, depending on the weather. The cap is a little frilly at the edges, like a lacy Victorian collar. Chanterelles are gathered in the wild, not cultivated, and sold at farmers' markets and specialty grocers. Their season depends on the weather, but generally it's late spring into early summer. Chanterelles are best eaten fresh; I don't find dried or powdered ones to retain much of their flavor. They are at once subtle with a delicate fruit flavor that some compare to apricots, lightly woodsy like the smell of wet maple leaves in fall, and slightly peppery.

Chestnut

Chestnut mushrooms, also known as cinnamon caps, have a beautiful brown-red color like their namesake nuts. They grow in clusters, both wild and cultivated, with frilly white scales that are present in the early stage of growth. Chestnut mushrooms are round in the cap, with long stems. (In the United Kingdom, the name "chestnut mushrooms" refers to the cremini variety.) Like beech mushrooms, they retain a bit of toothsome crunch even after cooking. Chestnut mushrooms have a nutty, peppery taste that pairs well with garlic and other umami flavors such as miso or seaweed. I find them to be very versatile mushrooms. Chestnuts are one of the easier and more popular types of mushrooms to grow in a home mushroom kit.

CANDY CAP

CHAGA

CHANTERELLE

CHESTNUT

CORDYCEPS

ENOKI

KING TRUMPET

LION'S MANE

COOKING WITH MUSHROOMS

Cordyceps

Cordyceps, sometimes referred to as caterpillar fungus, originate from Asia, and thrive in tropical forests and other areas with particularly humid conditions and high temperatures; they grow wild in the Himalayan foothills of Tibet and Bhutan. Cordyceps are now being cultivated successfully. They are bright orange or brown in color; their flavor is earthy and nutty, with some underlying bitterness. Cordyceps are prized for their adaptogenic properties. They are believed to help fight inflammation, boost oxygen and energy levels, enhance blood flow, and strengthen the immune system.

Enoki

Enoki mushrooms are delicate and thin, with long stems and tiny button caps. They grow in clusters, like long strands of mushroom grass. In the wild, they are native to many East Asian countries including China, Japan, and Korea, where they have a long-standing history in medicine. Wild enoki are exposed to the elements, so they are not as pure white as the cultivated varieties found in grocery stores; the cultivated ones are quite beautiful. Enoki have a very clean, mild taste with just a hint of sweetness; they are not deeply earthy. I like their crunch. I dehydrate enoki and use them to top Mushroom Chocolate Bark (page 211) and Salty Sour Dark Rye (page 73). Enoki are found year-round at specialty grocers, including Asian supermarkets. Prep enoki by trimming stem ends and separating the strands. I sometimes leave small clumps of them attached because I like the way they take on a fan-like appearance when cooked, as you can see in the Mixed Mushroom Pakora (page 154). Though they are often eaten raw, I prefer to sear or sauté enoki briefly before eating.

King Trumpet

With thick, hearty stems and narrow, flat, silvery-brown, trumpet-shaped caps, king trumpets are the largest mushrooms in the diverse oyster mushroom family. They are also known as king oysters or French horns. They grow wild in many places throughout the world and are also widely cultivated. Versatile king trumpets have a slightly sweet, earthy, woodsy flavor, becoming more deeply earthy as they cook (they have little to no aroma when raw). Once cooked, they can take on a meaty or seafood-like texture, depending on what they're cooked with. I use king trumpets to make a meatless au poivre (page 194) and a classic schnitzel (page 197). King trumpets are also nice when shaved super thin on a mandoline, then deep-fried and dusted with crunchy salt for super-umami chips (page 157) to serve with a creamy dip and cocktails. To prep king trumpets, trim off any woody stem ends; there won't be much else to clean, as they are usually free of dirt and debris.

Lion's Mane

Lion's mane is one of my favorite mushrooms. When found in the wild, they have long, icicle-like manes. Cultivated lion's manes are rounder and cloud-like, with tiny, needle-like hairs. They look quite otherworldly, like some made-up creature from beyond our universe. Some claim that lion's mane has a mild seafood flavor, while others liken it to cocoa. Yet saying that it tastes like crab or lobster does it a disservice, I think. The taste is much more complex, layered, and mysterious. Different flavor profiles come through based on cooking methods. When roasted, it's decidedly more seafood-like, but when dried into a powder, the effect is more rounded: earthy, intensely mushroomy, nutty, and buttery. You can find cultivated lion's mane year-round at specialty shops and grocers and from local growers at farmers' markets, or you can grow your own in a block kit. To prep lion's mane, I gently shred along the fiber into whatever size piece is needed; the mushrooms tear easily into crabmeat-like strands.

Maitake

I know I am not supposed to pick favorites, but if anyone is asking, maitake is mine, thanks to its fluffy, hen-like appearance. (It is also known as hen of the woods.) In Japan, it is called the dancing mushroom based on the folklore of the dancing joy felt when one is found. It is a dense, ruffled mushroom with frilly, overlapping stems and caps. Maitakes appear in beautiful, soft, striated browns, reminding me of a calico cat, the color running from a pale shade to a dustier deep brown, with thin dark edges around the cap. Maitake smells of the deep, cool forest, where it generally grows at the base of oak trees; the aroma is reminiscent of wet tree bark. Flavor-wise, it is woodsy and slightly funky, a little barnyard. Having grown up on a farm, I have an odd affinity for the smell of manure; maitake has this, in the same way that manure can smell sweet like hay and cows' breath. I add wildly earthy dried maitake powder wherever a dose of funky layered mushroom flavor is needed; it's the perfect savory to balance sweetness. Maitake is an adaptogenic mushroom with a long-standing history of use in Eastern medicine, boasting myriad health benefits.

Morel

Highly sought after and loved by chefs, morels are small, brown or yellow, honeycomb-like wild mushrooms that pop up in spring in the northeastern United States, as well as in Canada and Europe. Because they are not widely cultivated, they can be costly and considered a luxury food. Morels are intensely earthy, rich, nutty, and, in my opinion, a little mineral-y tasting. They are firm but spongy in texture. Because of their waffle-like exteriors and hollow stems and caps, morels must be thoroughly cleaned. Little critters like to hang out inside. Before cooking, shake them to expel sand or grit, then brush from top to bottom, reaching into each crevice (cut them in half if you want to really get inside). Morels are often found dried in small packages alongside other popular dried varieties such as porcini. Dried morels can be gritty, so I always soak and drain them in a fine-mesh sieve before adding to recipes. I don't use morel powder much; the earthiness doesn't come through as much as it does with other powdered mushrooms. Look for fresh morels in spring, but act fast—their seasonal window is fairly short, and you'll have to wait another year to enjoy them.

Matsutake

Matsutakes are among the most prized—and pricey—varieties of mushrooms. The flavor is spicy and intense; some describe it as smelling like old socks, while others compare it to cinnamon candies. These large mushrooms are elusive, growing only in very specific conditions, and are highly sensitive to changes in temperature and other weather patterns. Since matsutakes are most often found among pine trees, they have developed the nickname "pine mushrooms." The window for hunting and harvesting them is fleeting, so when one lucky forager comes across a bunch of matsutake, there can be a frenzy among those wanting to share in the bounty. Because of their expense, I use matsutakes sparingly in recipes. I like to dry and powder fresh ones, and then use a pinch or two to amp up the flavor of powdered blends that I sprinkle on all kinds of savory dishes; a tiny bit goes a long way.

Oyster

Oyster mushrooms are a diverse bunch. They come in many gorgeous colors, including canary yellow and seashell pink, oyster gray and silvery blue. The mushrooms generally grow in large, tiered, oyster-like clusters, with overlapping short stems and smooth, slightly curved large caps and exterior-facing gills. Oyster mushrooms are easily found in the wild, clinging to half-dead trees. Cultivated oyster mushrooms are widely available at farmers' and specialty markets, from local mushroom growers, and increasingly in grocery stores. They grow especially fast and are easy to cultivate with home kits or on logs or other substrate. I like to roast an extra-large cluster of oyster mushrooms as I would a chicken (see page 201). Oyster mushrooms are mild and versatile, frequently described as faintly woodsy or briny, kind of like a good oyster. Their texture is firm but soft and silky. If the mushrooms seem overly wet and develop any kind of ammonia-like smell, toss them! Oyster mushrooms take well to most cooking methods. Dried oyster mushrooms have a deep, woodsy, mineral-rich, salty flavor.

MAITAKE

MATSUTAKE

MOREL

OYSTER

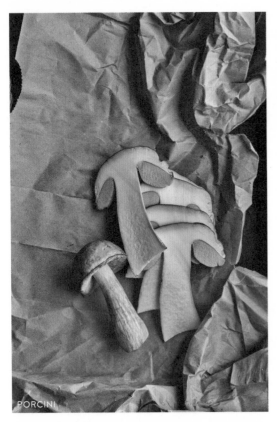

PORCINI

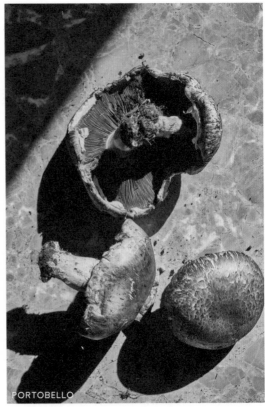

PORTOBELLO

REISHI

SHIITAKE

COOKING WITH MUSHROOMS

Porcini

This large-stemmed, reddish, rounded-capped mushroom, often referred to as cèpes or boletes, is beloved by chefs and gourmands. The thick pale stems often display an intricate web-like pattern. They have an aromatic, earthy, nutty flavor that intensifies greatly when dried. Fresh cooked porcinis are quite meaty in taste and texture. As they are only found in the wild and not yet cultivated, porcinis can be expensive. One mushroom gatherer told me the window for gathering them is quite small; if left in the woods too long, they quickly become slimy. Italians eat porcini raw in their famous salad with shaved parmesan and olive oil. I often dry porcinis. I find the dried powders to be a wonderfully aromatic addition to savory and sweet dishes.

Portobello

Portobello is the mature version of cremini and white button mushrooms. Its cap can sometimes be 5 to 6 inches (13 to 15 cm) wide, with dark, fluttery gills and flesh that is popular in all kinds of meatless recipes. Meaty, dense portobellos are more affordable than many specialty mushrooms; use them anywhere you would use creminis. They take well to most cooking methods, including searing, sautéing, and grilling, and are often stuffed, sliced into stir-fries, and grilled or broiled to make burgers. They work well in the recipe for Salt and Pepper Brick Mushrooms (page 202). Their flavor is relatively mild and not as complex as that of many of the wild varieties.

Reishi

Reishi is a polypore fungus, or "shelf mushroom." It has a single stem that attaches to dead or weakened hemlock trees, and a reddish brown to orange, kidney-shaped, slightly nubby cap that resembles a striated fan. The caps can grow as wide as 10 inches (25 cm) or more. When reishi is fresh, the texture is soft, woody, and cork-like; the flat cap is easy to slice through with a sharp knife or the blade of a small saw. The mushroom needs to be cut within 30 to 40 minutes of gathering, however, or it becomes too dense and difficult to penetrate. Reishi are not edible unless they are dried and powdered; their flavor is earthy and bitter. Reishi mushrooms have a long history as a medicinal mushroom in Eastern medicine. They are adaptogenic, helping to boost immunity and energy, reduce stress, lower cholesterol and high blood pressure, and improve sleep. Reishi is often made into a tea or tincture. I sometimes add the powder to broths and honey (page 58) to make the most of its adaptogenic properties. If you find reishi powder that's unrefined, with a texture like sawdust, grind it a little finer before using.

Shiitake

Among the most well-known mushrooms, shiitakes are popular all over the world, and now widely cultivated on rotting logs and other substrate. They have round, umbrella-like caps that are darker than the stems. Cap sizes vary in width from small to quite large, with deep, wide gills. Shiitakes taste more earthy and umami-like than white button and cremini mushrooms, yet the flavor is not quite as intense as that of many wild varieties. They are sometimes described as slightly smoky, with a chewy, dense texture. Donko shiitakes feature large, thick caps with a mottled brown and white pattern that gives them the nickname "flower mushrooms." They look as though they have grown too large for their skin and split in places. Donkos are dense, meaty, and sweet. Any variety of dried shiitakes can be used in broths (including ramen), soups, and stews. You will most likely want to separate shiitake stems and caps, depending on your recipe. The stems are tough and take longer to cook; reserve them for stock.

Truffle

Truffles, the ancient, mysterious, odiferous fruiting bodies of an underground fungus, are considered a delicacy. They are among the most expensive foods in the world. As such, they are highly coveted, bringing a fair fortune to those who find and sell them. Truffles can be black, white, or yellow ocher in color, and range in size greatly. Their exterior skin is coarse and scarred like a gnarled burl on an old tree or a very small knot of chaga. Inside, they have the most intricate and beautiful wood grain–like appearance. Traditionally, pigs and dogs are used to sniff out the prized truffles from the earth when they come into season in fall and winter. Truffles are impossible to store for any great length of time, as they lose their uniquely intense smell very quickly after being dug up. If you happen to get your hands on a fresh truffle, use it up quickly.

Turkey Tail

Turkey tail, one of the easiest and most common mushrooms to identify, is tough and woody. In the wild, it typically grows on fallen logs from late spring to early fall; it is also cultivated. Its striated appearance reminds me of a beautiful Missoni print. To be consumed, turkey tail is first dried or powdered and then steeped and added to teas, broths, and soups. While it does have a look-alike, true turkey tail is easily distinguishable from false turkey tail.

White Button and Cremini

Small, plump white buttons and meaty, dense brown cremini, their more mature form, are two of the world's most popular mushroom varieties. Both are widely cultivated and available year-round in supermarkets and grocery stores. These culinary workhorses are easily adapted to most any mushroom recipe. White buttons taste a lot milder than what you will find in wild varieties; I prefer the deeper, more earthy flavor of cremini. White buttons and creminis are commonly sliced raw and served in salads or scattered over pizzas, but they become especially flavorful when bloomed in fat or oil, whether sautéed, roasted, or grilled on skewers. The stems and caps are both edible and can be cooked intact or separated; you can chop up the stems to make a filling for the caps, as my grandmother did.

Wood Ear

Also known as jelly ear, cloud ear, black fungus, and tree ear, wood ear is a popular mushroom in Eastern cooking. It is a small, brown-black mushroom that looks a bit like an ear, hence the name. It is very mild, chewy, and somewhat slippery when cooked, resembling the texture of kombu. You can find fresh and dried wood ears at specialty shops and from Asian grocers. I use dried wood ears in the dashi for Maitake Ramen (page 147).

TRUFFLE

TURKEY TAIL

CREMINI AND WHITE BUTTON

WOOD EAR

THE MUSHROOMS

COOKING WITH MUSHROOMS

NOTES ON DRIED MUSHROOMS

Wild and cultivated mushrooms are easy to dry by a variety of methods. Most of the time, I slice mine thinly with a very sharp knife and put them into a dehydrator, but sometimes I lay them out to dry on a screen. I gently tear oyster, maitake, and lion's mane mushrooms in long, thin strips. Depending on the weather (if it is very humid, for instance), I sometimes put a fan on the mushrooms or use a clip light to speed the air-drying process. You want the mushrooms to be cracker-dry before you put them up for storage. When I first started drying my own, our children's friends considered us pretty peculiar, with mushrooms drying all over the place. For the most part, though, I think they kind of liked it, especially when I made them late-night pizza or breakfast pizza with mushrooms and a fried egg on top! They are willing to put up with almost anything for pizza.

Some mushrooms dry and store better than others. A few of the varieties that dry best for me are king trumpet, yellow foot (a type of chanterelle), maitake, porcini, chestnut, lion's mane, and oyster mushrooms. (See How to Dry Mushrooms, page 38, for instructions on drying your own.)

On Soaking

Dried mushrooms should be soaked in water to rehydrate them. Some varieties need to soak longer than others. Once the mushrooms have plumped up from the water, gently spoon them out of the liquid and give them a quick rinse. Set them aside until you're ready to use them in your recipe. Strain the reserved mushroom soaking liquid through a fine-mesh sieve or piece of cheesecloth to remove any bits or grit. Save the water that you soak the mushrooms in. Never throw it away—its flavor is gold! Use the liquid to flavor soups, broths, and risottos.

On Shopping

When buying dried cultivated mushrooms, always look for organic options. I have come to rely on a few favorite sources for dried mushrooms. Far West Fungi in the Bay Area has an excellent selection. See the Source Guide (page 232) for more dried mushroom purveyors.

On Storing

Store dried mushrooms and powders in a cool, dark place in your pantry, away from heat or light. Once you've opened them, seal the packages tightly.

On Powders

Any edible mushroom can be dried and buzzed into a powder. Single-variety and mixed blends are widely available in health food stores and from online suppliers, thanks to their well-documented health properties and benefits. Many mushrooms are loaded with antioxidants and adaptogens; the list of nutritional benefits varies by type. Some varieties, like chaga and reishi, are believed to boost energy levels and stamina, while others, like lion's mane, are thought to improve brain function.

Throughout this book, I use powders in savory and sweet dishes. I usually make my own at home, as it's much more economical than buying them. It is also a good way to stretch the life of fresh mushrooms when I just can't keep up with the sheer volume I end up buying at the market or getting from friends. (See How to Make Mushroom Powder, page 42.)

HOW TO DRY MUSHROOMS

I dehydrate and dry many herbs, vegetables, fruits, and, of course, mushrooms year-round. It's an easy way to extend the seasons. My dehydrator works overtime during spring, summer, and fall. This year-round process is a huge part of my kitchen larder. I dehydrate ramps, spring garlic, nettles, and garlic mustard in spring, which I then store, ready to be ground into a fine powder to dust on mushrooms or roasted vegetables, or add to broths, soups, stews, and creamy dips. In the summer, I dry herbs, including garlic chives, as well as edible flowers and tomatoes.

Dehydrated mushrooms are a must-have for any home kitchen. While cultivated mushrooms are more readily available year-round, farmers' markets carry wild mushrooms only when in season. Grab them while you can! Drying the varieties with short seasonal windows is a great way to preserve these flavor bombs. The dishes you can dream up are endless once you have an array of dried mushrooms on hand. A pound (about half a kilogram) of fresh mushrooms reduces greatly once dried, but the flavor only intensifies. With mushrooms specifically, dehydrating brings out a deep umami flavor. Umami is the fifth taste, the other four being sweet, salty, sour, and bitter. The direct translation from Japanese is "the essence of deliciousness" or "a savory pleasant taste." Dried, umami-rich mushrooms can be used to flavor broths and stocks, added to baking recipes, or buzzed to a fine powder and used as you would use a spice.

Shanxi Province

I first saw mushrooms drying in great abundance in northern China, in Shanxi Province. We stopped for some tea at a tiny morning market, where the women had piles of wild mushrooms laid out on cloth, drying in the morning sun. They'd collected them from the peaks of Wutai Mountain, a luminous, foggy, pine- and temple-covered wonder. Though I didn't speak their language, the women managed to explain to me perfectly their continuous pilgrimage to collect the mushrooms from the mountain during the different seasons. I will never forget the experience—it was such a beautiful moment. Inspired by these women, I dried many wild mushrooms in the summer and fall when I returned home. I was really happy with my first attempt and the pantry of little treasures that resulted.

If you cook a lot with mushrooms, you may have accidentally dehydrated some mushrooms by leaving them in a paper bag in the refrigerator or on your counter for too long. If this happens, do not throw them out! As long as they are bone dry, they can be stored for later use. I dehydrate mushrooms in a dehydrator for consistency and temperature control, but you can also air-dry them on a screen if you prefer. The key to air-drying is to promote good airflow all around the screen. I have also dehydrated on a sheet pan lined with parchment, placed in the oven on the warming setting. When the mushrooms are cracker-dry, I put them up in sealed glass jars for storage. Stored properly, away from heat and light, dried mushrooms should keep for several years. Some experts advise placing dehydrated mushrooms in the freezer. I like to use them in soups, stews, and countless other recipes.

COOKING WITH MUSHROOMS

DEHYDRATOR DRYING

Thinly slice or tear cleaned and trimmed mushrooms and lay them in a single layer on the dehydrator trays; if they are small (like morels, chanterelles, or shiitake caps), you can dehydrate them whole. Set the dehydrator to 125°F (52°C); they are ready when they are cracker-dry. When fully dried they should snap easily, like a cracker. Once they have cooled completely, transfer the dried mushrooms to a sealed glass canning jar for long-term storage.

How to Dry Leeks

You will see I call for dried leeks (pictured left) quite often in this book. I always have them on hand, since they add loads of flavor to soups and stews, brothy beans, eggs, and dips. I dry them the same way I dehydrate mushrooms, in a dehydrator or in the oven on the lowest setting. I thinly slice the leeks and wash them thoroughly. Then I set them on the dehydrator screens or sheet pans. Keep a close watch on them; they dehydrate faster than the mushrooms. Once the leeks are completely crisp and dry, store them in a sealed glass jar in a cool, dark spot in your pantry. They should last for up to 1 year. If you like, add a small, food-safe silica packet to keep them from absorbing any moisture during storage.

OVEN DRYING

Thinly slice or tear cleaned and trimmed mushrooms and lay them in a single layer on a parchment-lined baking sheet; if they are small (like morels, chanterelles, or shiitake caps), you can dehydrate them whole. Set your oven to a warming setting, the lowest setting possible (usually 170°F/75°C). Dry the mushrooms for several hours, flipping them occasionally, until they are cracker-dry. Keep your eyes on them, checking them often; depending on the temperature of your oven, they may dry more quickly than you think. Remove them from the oven, let cool completely, and transfer to sealed glass jars for long-term storage.

SCREEN AIR-DRYING

Thinly slice or tear cleaned and trimmed mushrooms and lay them in a single layer on a screen; if they are small (like morels, chanterelles, or shiitake caps), you can dehydrate them whole. Place the screen on small blocks or stacked books at the corners to allow the air to circulate all around the mushrooms. The mushrooms will take several days to dry this way. Mushrooms are very susceptible to humidity and will take on moisture like a sponge. If the weather is very humid, air-drying might not work and the mushrooms will never reach that desirable cracker-dry state for grinding into powders.

HOW TO MAKE MUSHROOM POWDER

If there is one big takeaway from this book, it is to make your own mushroom powders. They will transform your cooking. Once you have the powders on hand, you can experiment and add them to any dish as you would any spice. I keep a variety of mixed mushroom powders in my refrigerator or freezer (or a cool, dark cabinet) at all times. They are made primarily of cultivated varieties with some wild porcini or matsutake thrown in if I am lucky enough to get some. As with any dehydrated ingredient, the mushroom flavors are much more concentrated than when fresh. It's convenient to keep a mix on hand to use for risotto or ragu, or when baking bread, making granola, or mixing a mushroom latte. I buy all different kinds of mushrooms as I see them all year long. If I don't use them, then I simply dehydrate them (see How to Dry Mushrooms, page 38).

When I accumulate enough dried mushrooms, I add them to a spice or coffee grinder and pulse until a fine powder forms. I sieve to remove the larger bits and keep pulsing until they are all powdered. The mix of mushrooms can be tailored to any type of mushroom you like. I make certain blends (see page 50) for specific uses, and I encourage you to be creative.

Once your mushrooms are cracker-dry, you can grind them into powders. I prefer to make fresh powders as I need them, but for the sake of accessibility and convenience, they can be made ahead of time in bulk.

I like the ease of adding powdered mushrooms to dishes because they boost flavor in a concentrated way. I am layering in another flavor profile without adding another textural component.

If you are making a bulk batch, try to powder your mushrooms right after dehydrating them, when they will be at their driest. Mushrooms love moisture; if you leave them out for even a day after dehydrating, and it is at all humid, they will soak up moisture and you will have to dry them all over again. As a side note, if you prefer to make your mushroom powder as you go and prefer the ease of having dried mushrooms in your pantry, just put any slightly moist ones on a sheet pan in the oven at the lowest setting for an hour or two, before you powder them.

To buzz the cracker-dry mushrooms to a fine powder, I use a small powerful coffee grinder or spice grinder. If need be, I sift them through a fine-mesh sieve, directly into a storage jar, and return any large pieces to the grinder to reprocess until all the pieces are powdered. As long as they are stored in well-sealed jars, away from heat and moisture, they should last for up to 1 year. (See Mixed Mushroom Powders, page 50.)

ALWAYS ON HAND
IN THE LARDER

2

IN MY PANTRY

Cooking great meals and shopping for fresh produce are easier when you begin by building out a well-stocked larder. There are things you'll see in this book over and over, the pantry staples that I reach for most, my so-called flavor bombs. For me, cooking is experimental and inspiring. I love testing out new-to-me flavor profiles, and am hoping these ingredients, some known and some perhaps unfamiliar, will inspire you as well. I have collected a nice variety of spices, preserved citrus, tinned fish, oils and vinegars, and other small ingredients from my travels for work. You may wonder how these things pair with mushrooms, but I can tell you that they pair infinitely well in all kinds of creative ways. Mushrooms are incredibly versatile in texture and flavor, their inherent umami-ness becoming layered and nuanced with the addition of other umami flavors and textures. I shop for most fruits and vegetables, including staple alliums like garlic, leeks, and shallots, locally and seasonally at the many farmers' markets here in New York and buy directly from farmers whenever possible. (See the Source Guide, page 232, for a list of suppliers.) Here are my essentials:

ALLIUMS: Garlic (fresh and fermented black), onions (red, yellow, and white), tons of leeks and shallots, scallions, chives

BEANS, DRIED: I like Rancho Gordo brand, or I buy dried beans from the farmers at the market.

BONITO FLAKES: Smoked, fermented, shaved tuna (also known as katsuobushi)

BUTTER: Good salty butter, unsalted butter for baking, and ghee

CAPERS: I use salt-packed capers as well as capers in brine or in oil.

CHILES: Dried chiles de árbol, chile flakes, Aleppo pepper, and Kashmiri chile (ground and flakes)

CITRUS: Fresh limes and lemons (usually Meyer lemons), preferably organic, as the zest is often used, and salt-preserved (generally homemade during citrus season; see page 94), plus fresh Cara Cara oranges, Oro Blanco grapefruit, and yuzu (or store-bought yuzu juice when I can't find fresh fruit)

COCONUT: Dried shredded (unsweetened) and frozen fresh flakes

DAIRY: Cultured buttermilk, crème fraîche, heavy cream, and yogurt and labneh (often homemade), all organic and made from whole milk

COOKING WITH MUSHROOMS

DRIED FLOWERS: Organic and pesticide-free wild rose petals, chamomile, and hibiscus

EGGS: Organic, happy eggs, size large

FISH SAUCE: Colatura di alici—an Italian fish sauce that is described as the essence of anchovy in liquid form—is my secret umami weapon when it comes to savory cooking. I also use Red Boat fish sauce.

FLOURS: Organic whole-grain (rye, spelt, einkorn, buckwheat), acorn, chickpea, almond, and Italian "00" flours

GRAINS: Rice—Arborio, basmati, jasmine, and Forbidden Rice (Chinese black rice)—poha (flattened rice), oats, rye flakes, and spelt flakes

HERBS: I keep copious amounts of whatever is fresh and in season, but I am particularly fond of mint and oregano. You will see them used often here.

MISO PASTE: I prefer dark barley (red) miso, but white is lovely, too. I also keep umami-rich miso powder on hand (see page 53).

NUTS: Almonds, cashews, pistachios (pink and green), walnuts, and wild nuts

OILS: Extra-virgin olive, neutral oil like safflower for cooking, coconut, avocado, and nut oils like walnut

OLIVES: Castelvetrano, Bella di Cerignola, black (oil-cured and brine-cured Kalamata)

PASTA AND NOODLES: Homemade pasta, good store-bought pasta (including bigoli, fresh lasagna sheets, linguine, and maltagliati), ramen, soba, and rice vermicelli

PICKLES: Homemade pickled ginger, turmeric, onions (see Juniper-Pickled Onions, page 93), coriander seeds, pink peppercorns, and cherry blossoms

SALT: My cupboards are stocked with different kinds of salts but my go-to for cooking is Himalayan pink salt. For finishing, I like flaky, crunchy Maldon, coarse sea salts (such as Italian fiore di sale and sale di Cervia), and Celtic grey salt.

SEAWEED: Kombu and dulse

SEEDS: Chia, flax, hemp, pumpkin, sesame, and sunflower

SPICES: I buy single-origin, small-batch, sustainably sourced organic spices whenever possible, ideally from small farms. I tend to most regularly use turmeric (fresh and ground), ginger (fresh and ground), fennel seeds, cumin (seeds and ground), coriander (seeds and ground), curry leaves (fresh and dried), and saffron.

SWEETENERS: I prefer earthy maple syrup, jaggery powder (Indian palm sugar), molasses, date sugar, Japanese brown sugar, raw organic honey, cane sugar, and agave over refined granulated white sugar.

TINNED FISH: Sardines, boquerones (white anchovies), and jarred oil-packed anchovy fillets

TOMATOES: Good-quality canned San Marzano tomatoes and Sicilian strattu (concentrated tomato paste)

VINEGAR: Apple cider, rice, sherry, muscatel, and umeboshi plum vinegar, as well as home-made vinegars

WILD POWDERS: Nettle, pine, and spruce tip, ground at home or from specialty purveyors

MIXED MUSHROOM POWDERS

MAKES 1½ CUPS (60 G)

2¼ ounces (60 g) mixed dried
   (cracker-dry) mushrooms
   (specific blends follow)

Place the mushrooms in a spice grinder, mini food processor, or mortar and pestle and buzz or grind to a fine powder. Sift through a fine-mesh sieve to remove any large bits and return them to the grinder. Repeat the sieving and grinding until it's all a fine powder. Transfer to a sealed jar and store in the fridge or freezer. It should last indefinitely.

Everyday Mushroom Powder

¾ ounce (20 g) dried oyster
   mushrooms
¾ ounce (20 g) dried maitakes
¾ ounce (20 g) dried lion's manes

Use this all-purpose blend in Mushroom Ragu (page 186), Brown Butter Porcini Bagna Cauda (page 150), or any recipe that calls for mushroom powder.

Earthy Mushroom Powder

¾ ounce (20 g) dried maitakes
¾ ounce (20 g) dried shiitakes
¾ ounce (20 g) dried porcinis

This is perfect in recipes where I want to add a woodsy note, like any of the compound butters (page 54) or broths (pages 80–83).

Adaptogenic Mushroom Powder

¾ ounce (20 g) dried lion's manes
¾ ounce (20 g) dried reishi
¾ ounce (20 g) dried cordyceps (or
   chaga; but use 20 g powdered,
   because chaga is hard to grind)

I sometimes toss this mix into the granola (page 102) and the overnight oats (page 105) in place of the single-variety mushroom powders, or use it to make tea or a quick broth.

Mushroom Powder for Sweets

1 ounce (30 g) dried porcinis
1 ounce (30 g) dried candy caps

This is great in brownies (page 231) or crème caramel (page 215), or in any dessert where you want to add an especially fragrant note.

COOKING WITH MUSHROOMS

MUSHROOM SALT

MAKES 5 OUNCES (147 G)

¼ cup (22 g) dried (cracker-dry) mushrooms

½ cup kosher salt (Diamond Crystal), Himalayan pink salt, or Maldon salt

I love a nice earthy mushroom salt made with porcini, lion's mane, or the especially fragrant wild matsutake, but any type will do. Use the salt whenever you want to add a little extra mushroom flavor—on eggs and crudités, or to rim the glass of a margarita (page 166). Experiment with different types of salt; the grain size will affect the look and taste. Generally, I pulse the mushrooms with half the salt first, and then stir in the rest of the salt by hand, to preserve the integrity of the crystals. This way, the salt becomes more of a finishing salt. Play around and add some dried organic flowers or herbs, if you like.

In a food processor, combine the mushrooms and half the salt and pulse just until well blended. Remove and mix in the remaining salt by hand. This gives you a coarser salt texture; if you prefer a super-powdery salt, pulse all the salt and mushrooms together at once. (With Maldon, you can buzz the mushrooms to a fine powder and then stir them into the flaky salt crystals.) To make your salt with a mortar and pestle, first grind the mushrooms by hand until they are powder-like and then stir in the salt. The mushroom salt should last indefinitely stored in an airtight container at room temperature or in the freezer.

MISO POWDER

MAKES ½ CUP (63 G)

½ cup (135 g) miso paste (red or white)

Miso powder adds an extra salty funk, deepening the flavor of many recipes. I generally use a dark barley miso, but white miso works just as well. I use a dehydrator, since trying to dry the paste in the oven takes considerably longer and it sometimes sticks to the parchment paper. If you prefer to buy miso powder, see the Source Guide (page 232).

Using an offset or flexible spatula, spread the miso in a thin layer on a solid dehydrator tray. Place in the dehydrator set at 150°F (65°C) until dry but still pliable (it should feel like the texture of fruit leather), 4 to 5 hours. Break into smaller pieces and return to the dehydrator until cracker-dry, 1 to 2 hours more.

Break the dried miso into small pieces and buzz to a fine powder in a spice or coffee grinder. The powder should last in an airtight container in the refrigerator for up to 1 year.

MUSHROOM COMPOUND BUTTERS

Compound butters are so easy to make with fresh herbs, citrus zests, mushrooms, and other flavorings, and go a long way in preserving the seasons and adding depth of flavor to your cooking. I like to combine earthy mushrooms with lovage, garlic chives, nettle, and seasonal citrus. Try it anywhere you want a savory butter—with toast, scrambled eggs, pasta, steak au poivre (or King Trumpet au Poivre, page 194), roasted vegetables, pan-seared fish, or roast chicken. Well wrapped and frozen, the compound butters should last for up to 6 months. If you plan to serve the butter on its own, top it with a little flaky sea salt first.

Roasted Mushroom Butter

MAKES 4½ OUNCES (130 G)

1 cup (2½ oz/70 g) coarsely chopped or shredded fresh mushrooms, such as shiitake, maitake, lion's mane, or chestnut
1 tablespoon extra-virgin olive oil or ghee
Pinch of Himalayan pink salt
8 tablespoons (4 oz/115 g), cold unsalted butter, cut into 1-inch (3 cm) pieces
2 tablespoons chopped fresh herbs (optional; I like parsley and chives) or chopped lovage or nettles

Preheat the oven to 400°F (200°C).

Spread the mushrooms evenly on a baking sheet. Drizzle with the oil, sprinkle with the salt, and toss to combine.

Roast until soft, 10 to 15 minutes. Let cool completely.

Transfer to a food processor with the cold butter. Pulse until the ingredients are combined and the mixture is light and fluffy. Stir in the herbs, if using. If not serving immediately, wrap the butter in parchment paper or plastic wrap and tightly seal before transferring to the refrigerator or freezer.

Dried Mushroom Butter

MAKES 10 TABLESPOONS (135 G)

½ cup (¾ oz/20 g) dried (cracker-dry) mushrooms
8 tablespoons (4 oz/115 g) butter, cut into 1-inch (3 cm) pieces, at room temperature

In a food processor, pulse the mushrooms to a fine powder. Add the butter and pulse until the mixture is combined and light and fluffy. If not serving immediately, wrap the butter in parchment paper or plastic wrap and tightly seal before transferring to the refrigerator or freezer.

MISO MUSHROOM PASTE

MAKES ½ CUP (150 G)

½ oz (15 g) mixed dried (cracker–
dry) mushrooms, any variety
½ cup (135 g) red miso paste

When you combine dried mushrooms with miso, you get a double umami bomb. With only two ingredients, this larder staple is easy to make and to keep on hand. I add it to stocks and broths (it is an essential ingredient in Maitake Ramen on page 147), and even sweets like the 'Shroomy Nut Butter Chocolate Chunk Cookies (page 228). I prefer to use red miso, which is fermented with barley, over milder white or yellow miso, but, of course, use whichever you like. Once the mushrooms and miso are fully blended, transfer the paste to a glass jar and store in the refrigerator. If you have dried mushroom blends—like the Everyday Mushroom Powder or Earthy Mushroom Powder (page 50)—on hand, you can use ½ oz (15 g) in place of the dried mushrooms here and skip the buzzing step.

In a blender or food processor, buzz the mushrooms to a fine powder. Add the miso paste and process until the mushrooms are incorporated and the mixture is smooth. Transfer to a glass jar and refrigerate until ready to use. It should keep indefinitely.

MISO MUSHROOM BUTTER

MAKES ½ CUP (135 G)

8 tablespoons (4 oz/115 g) unsalted
butter, cut into 1-inch (3 cm)
cubes, at room temperature
1½ tablespoons Miso Mushroom
Paste (above)

My favorite way to use the miso mushroom paste is to mash it with room-temperature butter until soft and smooth using a mortar and pestle—or if I am feeling lazy, I buzz it in the food processor. I slather it on slices of Salty Sour Dark Rye (page 73), dollop it on roasting cauliflower, and bathe a roast chicken (page 177) in it at least once a week. Confession: A quick snack when I want a little bite and there is nothing much in the house is toasted rye with miso mushroom butter, a shaving of parmesan, and a drizzle of honey. It satisfies all the cravings.

In a food processor, combine the butter and miso mushroom paste and pulse until the mixture is smooth. If using a mortar and pestle, mash together the butter and mushroom paste until fully incorporated. Transfer to a sealed glass jar and refrigerate. The butter should keep in the refrigerator for up to 2 weeks, or up to 4 months in the freezer.

ADAPTOGENIC MUSHROOM HONEY

MAKES ABOUT 2 CUPS (480 ML)

2 cups (480 ml) raw organic honey
1 tablespoon lion's mane powder
1½ teaspoons chaga powder
1 teaspoon cordyceps powder
1 teaspoon maitake powder
1 teaspoon reishi powder
1 teaspoon ground ginger
1 teaspoon ground turmeric
¼ teaspoon ashwagandha powder
¼ teaspoon fennel pollen
10 saffron threads
Pinch of Himalayan pink salt
A turn of cracked black pepper
  (less than ⅛ teaspoon)

Delicious spread on toast, drizzled over yogurt, or stirred into your favorite tea, this magical honey is full of antioxidants as well as anti-inflammatory and immune-boosting properties. Have a spoonful when you're feeling under the weather or every day just to feel good; a spoonful before bed helps me sleep. The honey changes in color from clear golden to a darker, more opaque, nut butter–like shade when mixed with the other ingredients.

I used dried mushroom powders rather than fresh mushrooms, to avoid any fermentation in the honey. It is especially important to choose organic powders and spices, to avoid pesticides in your honey. The underlying earthiness from the chaga and the bitterness of the ashwagandha are tempered by the sweetness of the honey. A hint of fennel pollen adds a floral note, and cracked black pepper activates the turmeric.

Place all the ingredients in a 1-pint (480 ml) glass jar and stir to combine. Seal with a lid and refrigerate. Let it sit for 1 week to infuse before eating. The honey should keep for up to 6 months.

Note: Adaptogenic is a super-buzzy word these days. How does it relate to mushrooms? Adaptogenic mushrooms, very simply, are food as medicine. Mushrooms are an anti-inflammatory (inflammation is a leading cause of disease), antioxidant, and immune-boosting superfood. And taking mushrooms for their health-promoting properties makes so much sense to me, as I prefer to eat my medicine rather than take it in a pill, which always seem to come with side effects. People in Eastern countries and indigenous peoples around the globe have been eating mushrooms for their health for thousands of years. From teas to chaga-chinos to soups and smoothies—everything suddenly includes adaptogenic mushrooms! I like to go old school and make a slow-cooked, nourishing, rich broth that I can sip on all day as an elixir or add to countless other recipes. You will find staple broths on pages 80–83 to help keep your immunity boosted and your stress in check. Which mushrooms are considered adaptogenic and how do you take them? I stick to a few well-researched kinds, including reishi, chaga, cordyceps, lion's mane, shiitake, and turkey tail. With the exception of chaga, which is found exclusively in the wild, they can be wild or cultivated. Lion's mane and shiitake are the easiest to find at your farmers' market or grocer. Though both reishi and cordyceps are being cultivated, they are a bit harder to track down fresh; however, both are available powdered or dried. Reishi and lion's mane may be the easiest to add to your diet, as they are two of the most delicious mushrooms.

'SHROOMY NUT AND SEED BUTTER

MAKES 2 CUPS (365 G)

2½ cups (300 g) cashews (or almonds, walnuts, or any other nut you prefer)

½ cup (70 g) sunflower seeds (or any other seed you prefer)

3 tablespoons Everyday Mushroom Powder (page 50), Earthy Mushroom Powder (page 50), or store-bought mushroom powder (lion's mane and porcini work well)

2 tablespoons nutritional yeast

½ teaspoon Himalayan pink salt

¼ cup (60 ml) extra-virgin olive oil

1 tablespoon maple syrup (optional)

I like to make my own nut butters because of the unique flavor profiles that come from using different nuts and seeds. My favorite is made from a combination of cashews and sunflower seeds. The cashews and sunflower seeds are soft and buttery and take well to the addition of mushroom powders. As the nut butter sits, the mushrooms will bloom into the oils of the nuts, intensifying the taste. Thanks to the mushroom powder and nutritional yeast, this version has an especially earthy flavor. I use it in the 'Shroomy Nut Butter Chocolate Chunk Cookies (page 228). Some fruit conserves work nicely with the flavor of mushrooms, like apricots. Try apricot jam with this nut butter in a big, drippy, irresistible take on the classic PB&J. With a couple of tweaks (no maple and the addition of chile paste, sesame oil, and lime), this works as a savory base for Maitake Ramen (page 147).

In a food processor, pulse the nuts and seeds until almost sandy in texture (this is the first stage in making nut butter), 3 to 5 minutes. It's important to let everything combine and break down before adding the other ingredients. Stop and let the processor cool for a minute while you scrape down the sides. Add the mushroom powder, yeast, and salt. Pulse for 10 minutes, stopping intermittently to scrape the sides. In this second stage the nut butter will stick to the sides of the processor bowl. Keep pulsing and scraping until the nuts or seeds start to liquefy and slap the edges of the bowl. At this point, add the liquid ingredients—oil and maple syrup (if using)—and keep pulsing until the nut butter is completely smooth. This whole process should take 15 to 20 minutes. Store the nut butter in an airtight jar or container in the fridge; it should last for up to a month or more.

CONFIT MUSHROOMS AND SHALLOTS

MAKES 1½ POUNDS (710 G)

½ pound (225 g) mixed fresh
    mushrooms (shiitake and
    maitake work well here, but
    the choice is yours)
2 medium shallots, halved
    lengthwise
1 fresh bay leaf or 2 dried
1 fresh oregano sprig
1 organic lemon, zest removed
    in large wide strips with a
    vegetable peeler
1 bottle (750 ml) extra-virgin olive
    oil (you will not use it all)

I became a confit convert while photographing Carla Lalli Music's first book, Where Cooking Begins, *which includes an entire section devoted to the technique. Since that time, I have been confiting anything and everything, so mushrooms naturally fell under the spell. Here I mix them with oregano and shallots, which mellow at a low temperature over a long cooking time. Try experimenting with a variety of mushroom types and aromatics and serve the confit on grilled or toasted garlicky sourdough, atop flatbread or pizza, brushed over focaccia, or mixed into pasta with anchovies.*

Preheat the oven to 250°F (120°C).

Thinly slice the shiitake caps (leave smaller ones whole), and gently tear the maitakes. Place the mushrooms in a small heavy-bottomed ovenproof pot (like a Dutch oven) or a cast-iron skillet. Add the shallots, bay leaf, oregano, and lemon zest, then pour in three-quarters of the oil (2⅓ cups/565 ml) to submerge everything.

Transfer to the oven and cook until the mushrooms and shallots are soft, 2 to 2½ hours.

Cool the confit completely and then transfer to a large glass jar with a lid. Store in the refrigerator for up to 4 months.

COOKING WITH MUSHROOMS

MUSHROOMS À LA GRECQUE

MAKES 1 QUART (970 G)

1 teaspoon coriander seeds

1 head garlic, halved horizontally

1 cup (240 ml) red wine vinegar or
    apple cider vinegar

¼ cup (60 ml) unseasoned rice
    vinegar

2 tablespoons honey

1 shallot, thinly sliced lengthwise

1 cup (240 ml) wine (orange, white,
    or rosé)

Finely grated zest and juice of
    3 lemons, preferably organic

½ cup (120 ml) extra-virgin olive oil

10 to 12 saffron threads

1 chile de árbol, crushed

1 large bay leaf

1 tablespoon Himalayan pink salt

1 pound (455 g) cremini mushrooms
    (or any other variety), trimmed
    and quartered

8 fresh oregano sprigs, leaves
    picked

À la grecque, a French culinary term meaning "Greek style," is a very easy, quick way to cook vegetables by braising them in a flavorful vinaigrette, which slightly pickles them. I stick to a classic base here, with a few twists, including two vinegars plus lemon juice and zest, along with olive oil, a little wine, fresh garlic, and a few spices (saffron, coriander, bay leaf, and chile). It reminds me of the pickled white button mushrooms from every antipasto platter of my youth, but instead of being squeaky and squishy, these are fresh, vibrant, tart, garlicky, and nicely nuanced. Serve them on top of the Mushroom Frittata (page 113) or to amp up your own antipasto or cheese plate.

In a small cast-iron skillet over low heat, toast the coriander seeds until fragrant, about 1 minute. Remove from the pan and crush slightly with the side of a chef's knife.

In a nonreactive medium pot, combine the crushed coriander, garlic, both vinegars, the honey, shallot, wine, lemon zest, lemon juice, oil, saffron, chile, bay leaf, and salt. Bring to a bare simmer over medium-low heat.

Toss in the mushrooms and oregano, reduce the heat, and simmer until the mushrooms are soft, about 10 minutes. Remove from the heat and let the mixture cool completely in the liquid.

Transfer to a glass jar with a lid. Cover and store in the refrigerator for up to 1 week.

RUSTIC MAITAKE LOVAGE WALNUT PISTACHIO PESTO

MAKES 4 CUPS (528 G)

1 pound (455 g) fresh maitake
   mushrooms
¼ cup (30 g) pistachios, coarsely
   chopped
¼ cup (30 g) walnuts, coarsely
   chopped
1 tablespoon coriander seeds
3 tablespoons plus ¾ cup (180 ml)
   extra-virgin olive oil, plus more
   for topping
¼ teaspoon Himalayan pink salt,
   plus more to taste
3 garlic cloves, finely grated with
   a Microplane
¼ preserved lemon, store-bought
   or homemade (page 94), seeded
   and finely chopped
Finely grated zest and juice of
   1 lemon, preferably organic
¾ cup (25 g) fresh lovage or celery
   leaves, coarsely chopped
¾ cup (25 g) mixed fresh herbs,
   such as parsley, oregano,
   chives, and mint, coarsely
   chopped
½ cup (50 g) finely grated pecorino
   or parmesan cheese (I like the
   saltiness of pecorino)
Freshly cracked black pepper
½ dried red chile, such as chile de
   árbol, crushed (optional)

I made this rather untraditional pesto one summer when the garden was lush with overgrown lovage. I had some fresh maitakes and thought they would pair beautifully with the peppery leaves of the lovage, which has a celery-like appearance and a pronounced, slightly sharp taste and aroma—a little bit goes a long way. If you don't grow lovage and have a difficult time finding it, try a combination of parsley, tender celery leaves, and a little oregano in its place.

This pesto is earthy from the roasted mushrooms and bright from the preserved lemon. You can make it with other types of mushrooms, like lion's mane, shiitake, oyster, or chanterelle. Try the pesto on toasted slices of Salty Sour Dark Rye (page 73), tossed with pasta, or as a ravioli filling. Or spoon it onto sourdough toasts with shaved parmesan or pecorino or a thick smear of goat cheese. Use it to top pizza, flatbread, or focaccia, add a little to soft scrambled eggs (page 109), or simply stand over the jar and spoon into your mouth!

Preheat the oven to 400°F (200°C).

Gently shred the mushrooms into medium pieces.

On a large sheet pan or in a large cast-iron skillet, toss together the mushroom pieces, pistachios, walnuts, coriander seeds, and 3 tablespoons of the oil. Sprinkle with the salt and roast until crispy, 20 to 25 minutes, stirring halfway through.

Meanwhile, in a small bowl, combine the garlic, preserved lemon, lemon zest, and lemon juice and let sit to mellow the garlic.

Let the mushroom mixture cool, then coarsely chop by hand to preserve the texture and character of the mushrooms and nuts. (Do not use a food processor!)

In a large bowl, toss the lovage leaves and mixed herbs together. Stir in the remaining ¾ cup (180 ml) oil. Add the mushroom mixture, garlic mixture, cheese, and a hit of cracked black pepper and mix well to incorporate. Add salt to taste and the crushed chile if you want to give it a little heat.

If not using the pesto immediately, transfer it to a glass jar with a lid and top it off with a little extra oil to seal the top. The pesto should keep for up to 5 days in the refrigerator.

SEEDY MUSHROOM CRACKERS

MAKES ABOUT 1¼ POUNDS
(535 G)

Olive-oil cooking spray for the pan
1 cup (141 g) flaxseeds
½ cup (85 g) chia seeds
½ cup (85 g) hulled hemp seeds
½ cup (70 g) pumpkin seeds
½ cup (70 g) sesame seeds, black
     or tan
½ cup (70 g) sunflower seeds
3 tablespoons Everyday Mushroom
     Powder (page 50), Earthy
     Mushroom Powder (page 50),
     or any variety of mushroom
     powder
2 tablespoons nutritional yeast
¼ teaspoon Aleppo pepper
2 tablespoons psyllium husk
1¼ teaspoons flaky sea salt, such
     as Maldon, plus more for
     sprinkling
2 cups (480 ml) just-boiled water

We are a bit obsessed with flax crackers in our household, but the way they disappear is hard on the wallet. Let's face it: There aren't that many crackers in a box anyway and getting to the bottom of one is always disappointing. The good news is these gluten-free, seedy crackers are super easy to make. There are many versions of flax cracker in the world, but this one is loaded with mushroomy goodness thanks to a flavorful powdered blend.

Position a rack in the center of the oven and preheat the oven to 350°F (177°C). Lightly mist a half-sheet pan (13 × 17 inches/33 × 43 cm) with cooking spray and line it with a piece of parchment with a 2-inch (5 cm) overhang on each long side. Lightly coat the parchment with spray.

In a large bowl, combine all of the seeds, the mushroom powder, nutritional yeast, Aleppo pepper, psyllium, and salt, stirring to mix thoroughly until completely blended. Gradually pour the boiling water over the mixture, stirring well to combine after each addition before adding more of the water. Let sit until the dough becomes thick and the water is completely absorbed, about 10 minutes.

Transfer the dough to the lined pan. Using a flexible spatula, spread it into an even layer to cover the entire sheet pan, corner to corner. Sprinkle with salt. Press the salt into the dough with your hands and let the dough sit for 20 minutes.

Transfer to the oven and bake until the top is crispy and dry, about 1 hour.

Remove from the oven and let cool for 10 minutes (but leave the oven on). Using the parchment, lift the cracker from the pan, flip it over, and return to the pan (discard the parchment).

Return the pan to the oven and bake until crisp and dry, about 30 minutes longer. Transfer to a wire rack to cool completely in the pan before breaking into pieces. The crackers should keep in an airtight container in a cool, dry spot for about 2 weeks.

MISO MUSHROOM POPCORN DUST

MAKES ¾ CUP (75 G)

¼ cup (25 g) lion's mane powder
¼ cup (25 g) porcini powder
¼ cup (20 g) nutritional yeast
¼ cup (5 g) dried leeks (see page 41)
1 teaspoon miso powder, store-
    bought or homemade (page 53)
Popcorn, popped
Himalayan pink salt
Ghee or butter, melted

We are popcorn people in our house, so much so that years ago we dreamed up a family popcorn business. We tested out additions to our favorite popcorn (tossed with melted ghee and nutritional yeast), including dried herbs, seaweed, chile, turmeric, and miso powder. This is how the miso mushroom dust came to be. While we never managed to get our popcorn company off the ground, we still like to experiment. It seems everyone else had the same idea and the market is now flooded with specialty popcorn, but I promise this will become a family favorite. The miso mushroom dust has the bonus of being a great all-around mix to toss with roasted vegetables, spoon into thick yogurt or labneh for a dip, or rub or sprinkle over meat, poultry, or fish before cooking. If you have any homemade Mixed Mushroom Powder (page 50) in your pantry, try substituting an equal amount in place of the powders here. This quantity should last you for several batches of popcorn. Store in an airtight container in your freezer for optimal freshness. For serving, try using ½ tablespoon of dust per ⅓ cup (70 g) unpopped popcorn kernels.

In a food processor or spice grinder, buzz both mushroom powders, the nutritional yeast, dried leeks, and miso powder until combined. Sprinkle generously over popcorn. Add salt and melted ghee or butter to taste.

COOKING WITH MUSHROOMS

SALTY SOUR DARK RYE WITH MAITAKE AND LION'S MANE

MAKES 1 LARGE LOAF OR
2 SMALL LOAVES

LEVAIN

330 g (10½ oz) bubbly, active
    starter, fed in previous 6 to
    8 hours (see Feeding the
    Starter, page 76)
330 g (1¼ cups) filtered or
    chlorine-free water
330 g (2½ cups) organic dark
    rye flour

LOAF

Extra-virgin olive oil for the pan(s)
900 g (2 pounds) levain (above)
545 g (4½ cups) organic dark
    rye flour
409 g (1¾ cups) filtered water
25 g (1 tablespoon plus
    1⅛ teaspoons) Himalayan
    pink salt
13 g (2 tablespoons) lion's mane
    powder or crumbled dried
    (cracker-dry) lion's mane
    pieces
8 g (1 tablespoon) maitake powder
    or crumbled dried (cracker-
    dry) maitake pieces
18 g (3 tablespoons) nettle powder
    (optional)
135 g (1 cup) sunflower seeds or
    pumpkin seeds, plus more for
    topping (optional)
Dried enoki mushrooms (optional),
    for topping

A few years ago, I was bitten by the sourdough bug when I visited Riot Rye, a bakery in a self-sustaining eco-village in Ireland. The bakers there kindly shared their recipe with me and gave me a small plastic container of starter. Once home, I started tinkering with it, working on getting just the right amount of sour with 100 percent dark rye flour. After experimenting with longer and longer cold fermentation times, I developed an everyday loaf. Later, as I began incorporating powdered mushrooms into recipes, the bread was one of the first things I adapted. To be honest, one really good loaf is all you need, and I've landed on one with amazing flavor. Putting mushrooms in bread may seem unusual, but it's easy for anyone to experiment with, even with their own sourdough recipes. I have moved away from round loaves and started baking the bread instead in a pain de mie pan (also called a Pullman pan), which holds the shape of this wet dough better than a round pot. It's also easier to lop off a piece or two of the loaf to share with my family and friends or enjoy all by myself. I like it best toasted, with slightly burnt edges mingling with pools of melting salty butter and a good slather of Adaptogenic Mushroom Honey (page 58).

Make the levain: In a large ceramic bowl or other food-safe container, mix together the starter and water. Then mix in the rye flour. Cover tightly with plastic wrap and leave at room temperature for 24 to 48 hours to develop a pleasant fermented sour taste. (I like to leave mine for 48 hours before mixing the dough because I like super-sour bread.) You can experiment, and you may find 24 hours is your sweet spot. Taste it along the way, so you know how sour you like it. Remember, in warmer weather, the levain may ferment faster.

Make the loaf: Before measuring the ingredients, thoroughly coat a 2-pound (910 g) pain de mie loaf pan (about 13 × 4 inches/33 × 10 cm) or two 1-pound (455 g) loaf pans (about 9 × 5 inches/23 × 13 cm) with oil. Set them aside.

In a large clean bowl, combine the levain, rye flour, water, and salt, mixing with a wooden spoon or your hands. Add the mushroom powders (or crumbled mushroom pieces), nettle powder (if using), and seeds (if using).

When the dough is thoroughly mixed, let it sit for 10 minutes. It will remain a very wet dough; don't be alarmed. In order to handle it, you will have to wet your hands before transferring to the pan(s).

If you have one loaf pan, wet your hands and transfer the dough into it. If using two loaf pans, evenly divide the dough with your wet hands before plopping the dough into the two pans.

(continued)

Wet your hands again and smooth the top of the dough so that it is evenly spread in the pan(s). If you like, top with sunflower seeds or pumpkin seeds and dried enoki. Slide on the pain de mie cover or cover the pans with plastic wrap and let rest in the fridge to ferment for 24 to 48 hours, depending on your desired level of sourness. (I let mine ferment for the full 48 hours.)

Remove from the refrigerator and take the pain de mie cover or plastic wrap off. Cover with a tea towel and let proof for 2 hours in a warm (but not hot) spot.

Position a rack in the center of the oven and preheat the oven to 450°F (230°C).

If using the pain de mie pan, slide the cover on. Bake the smaller loaf pans for 45 minutes and the pain de mie pan for 1 hour. Remove the lid and bake for 15 minutes longer. To check for doneness, insert an instant-read thermometer in the center of the loaf; the internal temperature should be 190°F (88°C) or higher, and the bread should sound hollow when tapped on top.

Remove from the pan(s). Transfer to a wire rack to cool for 6 to 8 hours before slicing.

MAKING AND MAINTAINING A STARTER

This starter recipe is super easy to follow and comes with permission to share from my friends at Riot Rye Bakehouse in Tipperary, Ireland. They have developed a recipe for what they call The Common Loaf that uses a starter made with a mix of rye and whole-meal flour. I have adapted this to use exclusively rye flour for a 100% rye starter (with an equal weight of water, or 100% hydration).

If you would like to learn more about Riot Rye Bakehouse, see the Source Guide (page 232) for links. And you can check out their recipe for The Common Loaf at riotrye.ie/courses/the-common-loaf.

RIOT RYE STARTER

This starter takes 1 week to develop and then will last in perpetuity.

You will need:

1. A 1-quart (1 L) container with lid (A canning jar is perfect; however, do not seal the jar as carbon dioxide is produced during fermentation and needs to escape. If the container you choose is too wide, during the initial stages the starter may spread too thinly and inhibit fermentation.)
2. Kitchen scale (digital preferably)
3. 325 grams organic whole-grain dark rye flour
4. 325 grams filtered water

Day 1

1. 25 grams organic whole-grain dark rye flour
2. 25 grams filtered water

In your container, mix the flour and water together so that there are no dry bits, cover with the lid, and leave in a warm (70° to 77°F/21° to 25°C) part of your kitchen. The wild yeasts and bacteria on the flour will then begin to ferment the flour. After a couple of days you should notice some air holes and a slight sour smell and taste.

Day 2

1. Leave it alone.

Day 3

You are now going to refresh your starter by adding more flour and water to it. As the fermentation process has begun, this addition will ferment more quickly.

1. 50 grams organic whole-grain dark rye flour
2. 50 grams filtered water

Mix the flour and water together so that there are no dry bits. Cover with a lid. Leave in a warm place (70° to 77°F/21° to 25°C).

(continued)

Day 4

As you build up the beneficial bacteria and wild yeasts, you do so by keeping one-third starter and refreshing it with one-third flour and one-third water. To prevent being overrun with (and having too much) starter, first you discard some.

1. Discard (or compost) 100 grams of starter, keeping 50 grams.
2. Add 50 grams organic whole-grain dark rye flour.
3. Add 50 grams filtered water.
4. Mix the flour and water together so that there are no dry bits, then cover with a lid.
5. Leave in a warm place (70° to 77°F/21° to 25°C).

Day 5

1. Discard (or compost) 100 grams of starter, keeping 50 grams.
2. Add 50 grams organic whole-grain dark rye flour.
3. Add 50 grams filtered water.
4. Mix the flour and water together so that there are no dry bits, then cover with a lid.
5. Leave in a warm place (70° to 77°F/21° to 25°C).

Day 6

You are now going to build up enough starter so that you can make your bread on Day 7.

1. Add 165 grams organic whole-grain dark rye flour.
2. Add 165 grams filtered water.
3. Mix the flour and water together so that there are no dry bits, then cover with lid.
4. Leave in a warm place (70° to 77°F/21° to 25°C).

Day 7

Proceed with the recipe, using 330 grams of this built-up starter. Retain 150 grams of the starter for your next bake.

Feed your starter regularly (see right) and next time you plan to bake.

Making more loaves

Repeat the process from Day 6.

Feeding the starter

For the weeks that you are not baking, feed your starter about once a week. For the weeks when you are baking, feed it more often, and at least 6 to 8 hours before you plan to bake.

    150 grams starter
    150 grams organic dark rye flour
    150 grams filtered or chlorine-free water
(chlorine kills natural yeast)

To feed the starter, weigh out the 150 grams of starter and discard (or compost) the rest. Put the starter in a large canning jar. Add the rye flour and water and stir completely. Scrape down the sides with a flexible spatula. Place a rubber band on the jar at the level of the starter (so you can see how much it grows). Place the jar somewhere warm but not hot where you can keep your eye on it. I leave this on the counter for 6 to 8 hours to get active and bubbly. At that point if I'm baking, the starter is ready to use. Or if I'm not baking that week and it's just a maintenance feeding, then I put the starter in the refrigerator.

MUSHROOM JERKY

MAKES 4 OUNCES (115 G)

1 pound (455 g) fresh mushrooms,
  such as maitake, king trumpet,
  oyster, or shiitake
¼ cup (60 ml) maple syrup
2 tablespoons dark soy sauce
2 tablespoons rice vinegar
1 teaspoon sesame oil
1 tablespoon nutritional yeast
1 tablespoon yuzu juice

Use any meaty mushroom to make this fungi-based alternative to beef or other animal protein jerky. My favorite is maitake, but other varieties work just as well with this technique. Once you learn the process, you can get creative with spices and riff on any number of flavor profiles.

Trim and tear the mushrooms into medium pieces (thinly slice king trumpets, if using).

In a medium bowl, stir together the maple syrup, soy sauce, vinegar, oil, nutritional yeast, and yuzu juice. Add the mushrooms and toss to coat evenly on all sides. Let the mushrooms marinate in the sauce for 30 minutes and up to 12 hours.

With a slotted spoon, transfer the mushrooms to a solid dehydrator tray and dehydrate at 150°F (65°C) until dry but still pliable and chewy, 4 to 6 hours (start checking the mushrooms at 4 hours).

The mushrooms can also be dehydrated on a baking sheet in the oven on the lowest setting (about 150°F/65°C, depending on your oven); this should also take 4 to 6 hours.

The jerky can be stored in an airtight container at room temperature for up to 5 days.

BROTHS TO MAKE YOU FEEL GOOD

The following broths are always in my refrigerator or freezer, for sipping like tea to start the morning, keeping me going in the afternoon, or boosting immunity. I also use them in many of the recipes I've collected in this book. To infuse the broths with the most flavor, tear or cut the mushrooms into pieces, to create as much surface area as possible. A note about salting stocks and broths: If you are consuming the broth right away, salt it to your preference. If you are using it later in another recipe, such as the risotto (page 174), ragu (page 186), or any other recipe where it cooks down, wait to add the salt. It will become too concentrated as it reduces if you salt it ahead of time.

Everyday Mushroom Broth

MAKES 10 CUPS (ABOUT 2.4 L)

1½ pounds (680 g) mixed
    fresh shiitake and cremini
    mushrooms
5 quarts (4.7 L) water, preferably
    filtered
Himalayan pink salt (optional)

This delicious multipurpose broth is made from commonly available mushrooms and no additional aromatics. Sip on it all day or use it for any of the recipes that call for broth. After cooking and steeping, the liquid becomes a beautiful chestnut brown, with a deep earthy flavor. I make this broth without adding salt; add it later to taste, if desired.

Trim and slice the shiitakes and quarter the creminis.

In an 8- to 12-quart (7.6 to 11.3 L) stockpot, combine the mushrooms and water. Bring to a boil over medium-high heat and continue to boil for 15 minutes.

Reduce the heat and cook at a bare simmer for 1 hour. Remove from the heat, cover, and let steep for 3 hours, until completely cool. Strain through a fine-mesh sieve, pressing on the mushrooms (discard, or compost, the mushrooms). If you plan to sip the broth, add salt to taste. If you will be using it later for cooking, skip the salt.

Transfer the broth to glass jars for storage. If freezing, leave ¾ inch (2 cm) of free space at the top of the jar for expansion. Refrigerate for up to 5 days or freeze for up to 6 months.

EVERYDAY MUSHROOM BROTH

LION'S MANE BROTH

GOLDEN TONIC ELIXIR WITH TURMERIC
MUSHROOMS AND BLACK GARLIC

ADAPTOGENIC SIPPING BROTH

ALWAYS ON HAND IN THE LARDER

Lion's Mane Broth

MAKES 10 CUPS (ABOUT 2.4 L)

1½ pounds (680 g) fresh lion's
    mane mushrooms
5 quarts (4.7 L) water
Himalayan pink salt (optional)

This clean broth is almost like a mushroom tea, with lots of delicate, buttery, nutty, earthy flavors. The broth is sometimes my preferred morning drink, trumping coffee. If I am working from home, I will heat up a quart (1 L) and sip it all day. I use it for the Brothy Mushrooms, Beans, and Greens (page 205), the Rice Porridge with Trout and Crispy Mushrooms (page 106), and the Leek-Mushroom Risotto (page 174).

With your hands or two forks, gently tear the lion's mane into small shreds.

In an 8- to 12-quart (7.6 to 11.3 L) stockpot, combine the shredded mushrooms and water. Bring to a boil over medium-high heat and continue to boil for 15 minutes.

Reduce the heat and cook at a bare simmer for 1 hour. Remove from the heat, cover, and let steep for 3 hours, until completely cool.

Strain through a fine-mesh sieve, pressing on the mushrooms (discard, or compost, the mushrooms). If you plan to sip the broth, add salt to taste. If you will be using it later for cooking, skip the salt.

Let cool completely, then transfer to glass jars for storage. If freezing, leave ¾ inch (2 cm) of free space at the top of the jar for expansion. Refrigerate for up to 5 days or freeze for up to 6 months.

Golden Tonic Elixir with Turmeric Mushrooms and Black Garlic

MAKES ABOUT 8 CUPS
(ABOUT 2 L)

1 pound (455 g) mixed fresh
    mushrooms, any variety (oyster,
    maitake, and shiitake all work
    well here)
6 quarts (5.6 L) water
2 large heads garlic, halved
    horizontally, unpeeled
2 to 3 black garlic cloves, smashed
    with the side of a knife, unpeeled
1-inch (3 cm) nub fresh ginger,
    sliced

For years, I was in the habit of making broth with the carcass left over from our weekly roast chicken. Last winter, my daughter requested a vegetarian version, so we transitioned to making it with mushrooms and included black garlic for earthy smokiness, and ginger and onion for their immunity-boosting properties. It is the perfect healing broth for sipping. I brighten with a squeeze of fresh lime just before serving.

Clean and trim the mushrooms. If using oysters or maitakes, shred into pieces. If using shiitakes, trim and leave the stems on.

In an 8- to 12-quart (7.6 to 11.3 L) stockpot, combine all the ingredients. Bring to a boil over medium-high heat and continue to boil for 15 minutes.

1 medium yellow onion, halved,
    unpeeled
2-inch (5 cm) nub fresh turmeric,
    finely grated with a Microplane,
    or 1 tablespoon ground
    turmeric
1 celery stalk with leaves (optional)
1 tablespoon Himalayan pink salt,
    plus more to taste
1½ teaspoons coriander seeds,
    crushed with the side of a knife
1½ teaspoons fennel seeds,
    crushed with the side of a knife
½ dried red chile, such as chile de
    árbol, crushed

Reduce the heat and cook at a bare simmer for 2 hours. Remove from the heat, cover, and let steep for 3 hours, until completely cool.

Strain through a fine-mesh sieve, pressing on the solids (discard, or compost, the solids).

Transfer the broth to glass jars for storage. If freezing, leave ¾ inch (2 cm) of free space at the top of the jar for expansion. Refrigerate for up to 5 days or freeze for up to 6 months. Add more salt to taste and a squeeze of lime juice before serving.

Adaptogenic Sipping Broth

MAKES 10 CUPS (ABOUT 2.4 L)

1 pound (455 g) fresh shiitake
    mushrooms
½ pound (225 g) fresh lion's mane
    mushrooms
3 long (4- to 5-inch/10 to 13 cm)
    pieces dried reishi mushrooms
¼ ounce (7 g) dried cordyceps
    mushrooms
¼ ounce (7 g) piece chaga (about
    the size of a walnut), or
    2 teaspoons (2 g) ground chaga
¼ ounce (7 g) piece dried turkey
    tail (optional)
5 quarts (4.7 L) water

This beautiful salt-free broth tastes so deeply delicious and is also good for you. All of the mushrooms in it—shiitake, lion's mane, reishi, cordyceps, chaga, and turkey tail—have medicinal and adaptogenic properties. Many of the vegetable and mushroom broths on the market are often cloudy and a little funky, but homemade broths are so clean, and they're perfect in any recipe calling for a vegetarian or vegan broth (and for anyone on a low-sodium diet).

Clean and trim the fresh mushrooms. Slice or tear them into small pieces.

In an 8- to 12-quart (7.6 to 11.3 L) stockpot, combine all the ingredients. Bring to a boil over medium-high heat and continue to boil for 15 minutes.

Reduce the heat and cook at a bare simmer for 1 hour. Remove from the heat, cover, and let steep for 3 hours, until completely cool.

Strain through a fine-mesh sieve, pressing on the mushrooms (discard, or compost, the mushrooms).

Transfer the broth to glass jars for storage. If freezing, leave ¾ inch (2 cm) of free space at the top of the jar for expansion. Refrigerate for up to 5 days or freeze for up to 6 months.

ACCOMPANIMENTS

The following recipes include many of the smooth and creamy or bright and tangy condiments and other tasty things I serve with multiple mushroom dishes.

Coriander Yogurt

MAKES ABOUT 1 CUP (230 G)

1 cup (225 g) whole-milk yogurt
Finely grated zest and juice of
    ½ lime, preferably organic
¼ teaspoon jaggery powder or
    brown sugar
¼ teaspoon Himalayan pink salt
1 teaspoon ground coriander

This super-versatile sauce is one of my favorites. It pairs perfectly with the Sweet and Sour Mushroom Pumpkin Curry (page 179) and any of the taco recipes beginning on page 132.

In a small bowl, combine all the ingredients and stir until smooth.

Green Goddess Dressing

MAKES 1 CUP (225 G)

1 cup (40 g) coarsely chopped
    mixed fresh herbs, such
    as parsley, mint, cilantro,
    tarragon, dill, and chives
½ cup (115 g) whole-milk Greek
    yogurt
Finely grated zest and juice of
    1 lemon, preferably organic
    Meyer lemon
1 tablespoon extra-virgin olive oil
2 white anchovies (boquerones)
1½ teaspoons capers, rinsed and
    drained
½ garlic clove, peeled
¼ teaspoon Himalayan pink salt
¼ teaspoon coarsely ground black
    pepper

There are about as many ways to make this dressing as there are to roast a chicken. This version includes white anchovies, capers, a little garlic, and, of course, lots of herbs. It's an easy dressing to quickly buzz up in the processor. Use it on the Mushroom Mint Summer Rolls (page 131) or on salad greens any time of year. Pictured left

In a food processor, pulse all the ingredients until well combined. Transfer to a small serving bowl.

Briny Yogurt Tartar Sauce

MAKES ABOUT 1 CUP (330 G)

½ cup (115 g) whole-milk yogurt
½ cup (80 g) coarsely chopped
    dill pickles or cornichons
¼ cup (30 g) coarsely chopped
    stemmed large caper berries
1 small shallot, finely chopped
1 small garlic clove, finely grated
    with a Microplane
1 tablespoon finely chopped
    fresh dill
1 tablespoon finely chopped
    fresh flat-leaf parsley
½ teaspoon mustard powder
Grated zest and juice of 1 lemon,
    preferably organic
¼ teaspoon Himalayan pink salt
A few turns of cracked black
    pepper

As a kid, I was not into tartar sauce, which usually accompanied some kind of frozen fish stick. I think it might have been the mayonnaise, which I really wasn't crazy about, even though it was often homemade. This version is made with whole-milk yogurt and a few of my favorite pickled things—namely, caper berries and pickles—not surprising, since I was the kid who asked for a half sour for her birthday. Garlic, herbs, and mustard powder round out this tangy little number. Serve it with the Brown Butter Mushroom Cakes (page 161).

In a small bowl, stir together all the ingredients until well combined.

Cilantro Mint Crema

MAKES ABOUT 2 CUPS (550 G)

1½ cups (360 g) Mexican crema
    or labneh
Finely grated zest and juice of
    3 limes, preferably organic
1 garlic clove, finely grated
½ cup (20 g) coarsely chopped
    fresh cilantro leaves and stems
½ cup (15 g) fresh mint leaves
¼ teaspoon Himalayan pink salt

Our taco nights are never complete without this creamy, pale-green sauce. The family favorite pairs beautifully with mushrooms, fish, or pork. I like to make it ahead and let the garlic, cilantro, and mint infuse the dairy.

In a food processor, combine all the ingredients and pulse until smooth.

ALWAYS ON HAND IN THE LARDER

COOKING WITH MUSHROOMS

Yuzu Chili-Garlic Soy Dipping Sauce

MAKES ½ CUP (120 G)

3 tablespoons tamari
1 tablespoon yuzu juice
1 tablespoon unseasoned rice
    vinegar
1 tablespoon chili-garlic sauce
Finely grated zest and juice of
    ½ Meyer lemon, preferably
    organic
1 teaspoon sesame oil
1 teaspoon honey
¼ cup (15 g) finely chopped
    scallions (optional)

I am crazy about yuzu, an especially fragrant citrus native to Japan and China. These days, there are farmers cultivating yuzu in the United States, too. I keep organic yuzu juice on hand at all times; it's easy to find at specialty grocers and Japanese markets. It adds a special floral citrus flavor, reminiscent of makrut lime, and is the secret ingredient in my dumpling dipping sauce. The season for fresh yuzu is fleeting, and they are hard to find even at specialty grocers. When I do find them, I preserve them like lemons (see Salt-Preserved Lemons, page 94). Pictured left

In a medium bowl, whisk to combine the tamari, yuzu juice, vinegar, chili-garlic sauce, lemon zest, lemon juice, oil, and honey. If desired, stir in the scallions.

Cilantro Mint Chutney

MAKES ABOUT 1 CUP (235 G)

1 teaspoon coriander seeds
1 cup (30 g) fresh cilantro leaves
    and stems, finely chopped
1 cup (30 g) fresh mint leaves,
    finely chopped
1 garlic clove, finely grated with a
    Microplane
Juice of 2 limes
⅓ cup (80 ml) water or whole-milk
    yogurt
2 teaspoons extra-virgin olive oil
½ teaspoon ground coriander
¼ to ½ dried red chile, such as
    chile de árbol, crushed, or
    ¼ teaspoon chile flakes
2 teaspoons jaggery powder or
    brown sugar, plus more to taste
¼ teaspoon Himalayan pink salt,
    plus more to taste

Every family in India has its own version of cilantro mint chutney. Some are ground on stone, while others are blended in a food processor. This one, which came together with the help of my dear friend Ayesha Patel, is hand-chopped for a coarser chutney made with water and lots of lime. You can use whole-milk yogurt in place of the water for a creamier chutney, if you like. If a smoother chutney is your jam, by all means toss everything into a food processor and pulse until smooth. Serve it with the pakora (page 154), the tostada (page 120), or any of the mushroom tacos (pages 132–139).

In a small dry cast-iron skillet over medium-low heat, toast the coriander seeds just until fragrant. Remove from the heat and let cool, then coarsely smash with the side of a chef's knife.

In a small bowl, combine the cilantro, mint, garlic, lime juice, water, oil, ground coriander, smashed coriander seeds, chile, jaggery, and salt. Add a little more water if you want to thin out the chutney before serving.

Mixed Herb Pesto

MAKES 2 CUPS (400 G)

4 cups (160 g) packed fresh herbs,
    such as basil, oregano, mint,
    or parsley
3 garlic cloves, smashed and
    peeled
¾ cup (180 ml) extra-virgin olive
    oil, plus more for storing
1 cup (100 g) finely grated pecorino
    or parmesan cheese
Finely grated zest and juice of
    2 Meyer lemons, preferably
    organic
¼ dried red chile, such as chile de
    árbol, crumbled
Himalayan pink salt

This is delicious with the King Trumpet Schnitzel (page 197), but use it anywhere you would use basil pesto—mixed into pasta with sautéed mushrooms, spooned over grilled mushrooms on toast, or in a sandwich. It's very versatile. Pictured right

In a food processor, pulse together the herbs and garlic to combine. Add the oil a little at a time and pulse just until combined.

Add the cheese and pulse until just combined (do not overprocess).

Remove the bowl from the machine and stir in the lemon zest, lemon juice, and chile by hand. Season with salt to taste. If not using immediately, transfer the pesto to a glass jar and top off with oil to prevent browning.

Double-Cumin Yogurt Dip

MAKES 1¼ CUPS (285 G)

1 cup (225 g) whole-milk yogurt
1½ teaspoons ground cumin
1½ teaspoons cumin seeds,
    toasted and crushed with the
    side of a knife
⅛ preserved lemon, store-bought
    or homemade (page 94), seeded
    and finely chopped
Finely grated zest and juice of
    1 Meyer lemon, preferably
    organic
1 garlic clove, grated with a
    Microplane
1 cup (30 g) fresh cilantro leaves,
    coarsely chopped
1 cup (30 g) fresh mint leaves,
    coarsely chopped

Dairy takes beautifully to rich herbs and spices, and this yogurt dip is no exception. The copious herbs, preserved lemon, and double hit of cumin make it especially flavorful. Serve it with the Shiitake Kofta (page 140), on eggs, as a dip for crudités, with tacos—basically, anywhere and everywhere!

In a food processor, combine all the ingredients and process just until smooth. Transfer to a small serving bowl.

Green Cabbage Slaw with Citrus and Celery Seed

MAKES 4 CUPS (360 G)

¼ head green cabbage, thinly
sliced with a mandoline or
sharp knife
1 tablespoon yuzu juice
3 tablespoons unseasoned rice
vinegar
1 teaspoon honey
1 teaspoon celery seeds
2 tablespoons extra-virgin olive oil
¼ teaspoon flaky sea salt, such as
Maldon, plus more to taste
3 tablespoons chopped fresh dill

*This citrusy slaw adds the perfect crunch, freshness, and brightness to
the King Trumpet Schnitzel (page 197); it's perfect with grilled fish and
chicken, too.*

In a medium bowl, toss together the cabbage, yuzu juice, vinegar,
honey, and celery seeds. Drizzle in the oil, then toss with the salt and
dill. Add more salt to taste, if desired.

Juniper-Pickled Onions

MAKES 1½ CUPS (360 G)

1 red onion or 2 small shallots,
thinly sliced lengthwise
½ teaspoon Himalayan pink salt
½ cup (120 ml) unseasoned rice
vinegar
½ cup (120 ml) apple cider vinegar
1 tablespoon maple syrup
4 juniper berries, crushed with the
side of a knife

*My kitchen is always stocked with these easy, bright-tasting pickles.
The two vinegars temper the bite of the raw onion (or shallots, which
work just as well), and the maple and juniper do a little fragrant
dance. Not only do we top our tacos with these pink beauties, but we
throw them on eggs, rice porridge (page 106), tostadas (page 120), and
anywhere we want a sharp-sweet bite. Pictured left*

Place the onions in a heatproof medium bowl. Sprinkle with the salt
and massage for 30 seconds. Set aside.

In a small saucepan, bring both vinegars, the maple syrup, and juniper
berries to a simmer over medium heat. Pour over the onions and
refrigerate for 10 to 15 minutes (or up to 1 day) before serving.

SALT-PRESERVED LEMONS

MAKES 1 QUART (1 L)

6 to 8 Meyer lemons, preferably
    organic
8 regular lemons, preferably organic
1 cup (230 g) kosher salt
6 to 8 bay leaves
Pink peppercorns (optional)

One of my favorite meditative activities on a quiet snowy day, deep in citrus season, is to preserve lemons. I usually start with Meyer lemons because they are a staple in my cooking and such umami bombs. Meyer lemons have thinner skins than regular varieties, so they soften in the salt more quickly. Play around with the herbs, spices, and heat you add. When the lemons are ready, try buzzing a few in the food processor; the thick, glossy paste adds salty, briny brightness to any dish.

Sterilize a 1-quart (1 L) glass canning jar.

Cut the Meyer lemons lengthwise into quarters, leaving them attached at one end. (Use as many lemons as you can fit in the jar.) Juice the regular lemons (you will need about 2 cups/480 ml juice).

Pack the interior of each Meyer lemon with salt. Add a bay leaf to each Meyer lemon and tuck the lemons into the canning jar. Add lemon juice to cover the lemons completely and tuck peppercorns (if using) into the jar.

Add a layer of plastic wrap before screwing on the lid. (The salt may start to eat away the metal lid over time; you don't want the jar to get rusty and spoil the lemons.)

Store the jar in a cool, dark place to allow the lemons to ferment for 1 month, shaking every other day or so. They will keep indefinitely. Refrigerate after opening.

3

MUSHROOMS IN THE MORNING

CHAGA CHAMOMILE TEA

MAKES ABOUT 4 CUPS (1 L)

7 ounces (200 g) small chaga
   chunks
1 small bundle fresh chamomile
   (about 7 stems) with flowers, or
   ⅓ cup (12 g) fresh chamomile
   flowers (heads only, no
   stems), or 2 tablespoons dried
   chamomile
8 cups (2 L) filtered water
Oat or nut milk of choice
Adaptogenic Mushroom Honey
   (page 58) or maple syrup,
   for serving

Chaga reminds me a little of maple sap. Its delicate, earthy sweetness is very light yet distinctly woody. I often use chaga powder in baking, or steep small pieces for hot or cold tea. When brewing it for tea, be careful not to boil the water, which would kill the beneficial medicinal and antioxidant properties of the fungus. You can add fresh herbs while it simmers; I like chamomile for its soothing properties and beautiful, flowery notes. Serve it hot or cold with frothy oat or nut milk and adaptogenic honey. You can sometimes find chaga at farmers' markets, but more often at a health food store or online. If you find chaga in the woods, remember to leave some on the tree. This is how it will reproduce and come back the following year.

In a small heavy-bottomed pot, combine the chaga, chamomile, and water. Bring to a gentle simmer over low heat. Do not boil! Let the mixture simmer very gently for 1 hour. The water should reduce by about one-third, no more than that; if it does, add more water.

Remove from the heat and let cool. Remove the chaga and chamomile with a slotted spoon—set aside the chaga to dry. (Chaga can be reused until the water in which you boil it stays clear. Store dried pieces in a glass jar in your cupboard.)

Enjoy the tea warm or chilled, as a morning or afternoon drink or as iced tea, with steamed milk of your choice and sweetened with honey or maple syrup.

SPICY CAROB MUSHROOM LATTE

SERVES 2 TO 3

2 cups (480 ml) milk of choice
    (I like oat)
2 tablespoons maple syrup
    (optional)
2 teaspoons carob powder
2 teaspoons mixed mushroom
    powder, any variety (I like a
    mix of lion's mane, cordyceps,
    and reishi), or the Adaptogenic
    Mushroom Powder (page 50)
1 teaspoon chaga powder
Teeny-tiny piece dried chile de
    árbol, crushed
Pinch of Himalayan pink salt

Carob is one of those ingredients that has a hippie, 1970s vibe, at least in my family. For years we ate it in place of chocolate, when we were off sugar and eating super-healthy whole foods. Back then carob was promoted as a chocolate substitute, but in my memory, it tasted nothing like chocolate. It has a flavor all of its own—a little dusty and a little nutty. While I may not be selling you on it, I promise that when it's paired with maple and mushroom, carob blooms into something delicious. Pour it over ice into a cocktail shaker with a shot of espresso and mix it up vigorously for an ice-cold carob-mushroom shakerato, an ode to the classic Italian café drink.

In a small heavy-bottomed pot, combine all the ingredients and warm over medium-low heat just until they reach a simmer. Cover the pot, remove from the heat, and let everything infuse for 15 minutes.

Strain through a fine-mesh sieve (the mushroom powder can be gritty, and you want to strain out any bits of chile as well).

Reheat over medium-low and steam with a milk frother or whisk vigorously until frothy. Serve warm.

MUSHROOM ROSE CARDAMOM RYE GRANOLA

MAKES 3 QUARTS (1.3 KG)

4 cups (400 g) organic rye flakes

1 cup (160 g) organic rolled spelt flakes

1½ cups (210 g) raw, unsalted sunflower seeds

5 organic cardamom pods, seeds removed and coarsely chopped

2 teaspoons maitake or matsutake powder

1 teaspoon cordyceps powder

1 teaspoon reishi powder

½ teaspoon white pine needle powder (optional)

1½ teaspoons Himalayan pink salt, plus more for seasoning

1 cup (240 ml) dark maple syrup

1 cup (240 ml) organic coconut oil, melted

1 cup (130 g) pistachios, roughly chopped

¼ cup (5 g) dried rose petals, organic and pesticide-free

I got into making granola a few years ago, largely because it was way more economical than buying it. I started to play around with flavor profiles and landed on this nutty, slightly salty mushroom-rye combination with the added adaptogenic health benefits of cordyceps and reishi. (If you want to experiment with flavors, try substituting the powders listed here with Adaptogenic Mushroom Powder or Mushroom Powder for Sweets, page 50.) I love pairing maple syrup with mushrooms, as they are both earthy; maple also tempers any bitterness from the mushroom powder and grounds the flavors. I include cardamom, rose, and pistachio as an ode to India, inspired by the Rajasthani desert with its colorful hits of hot pink, green, and scorched clay earth. I use a combination of pink and green shelled pistachios, but you can use whatever nut you like.

Preheat the oven to 350°F (177°C). Line a large sheet pan with parchment paper.

In a large bowl, combine all the ingredients except the pistachios and rose petals, tossing to coat. Spread into an even layer on the lined pan. Bake for 45 minutes to 1 hour, stirring every 15 minutes so it doesn't burn.

Transfer to a wire rack to cool. Once cool, toss the granola with the pistachios and rose petals. Taste for salt, adding a pinch or two more if desired. Store the granola in an airtight container at room temperature. It should keep for up to 4 months.

ADAPTOGENIC MUSHROOM OVERNIGHT OATS

SERVES 4

1 cup (90 g) whole-grain rolled
    oats, preferably organic
2 cups (480 ml) oat or nut milk (or
    whole milk or water)
¼ cup (30 g) coarsely chopped
    pistachios (or other nuts)
¼ to ½ cup (35 to 70 g) dried fruit
    (golden raisins, chopped dates,
    plums, or apricots)
2 tablespoons sesame seeds
5 threads saffron, plus a pinch,
    for topping
1 tablespoon lion's mane powder
1 teaspoon chaga powder
1 teaspoon red reishi powder
¼ teaspoon ashwagandha powder
2 tablespoons maple syrup, brown
    sugar, jaggery powder (or my
    favorite, Okinawan dark brown
    sugar), plus more for topping
Pinch of Himalayan pink salt
Fresh or dried fruit, for topping
Coarsely chopped nuts, for topping
Mushroom powder, any variety,
    for topping

A few years ago, after picking up some overnight oats at a juice spot near my home, I was immediately hooked. Rich, creamy, slow-cooked oatmeal reminds me of childhood mornings when breakfast was still a sit-down experience. The reality of most of my mornings now doesn't allow for the time to stand over the stove. With these soaked oats, I can quickly grab and go. The oats are easy to tailor for whatever seasonal ingredients I am into on any given week. I like tart rhubarb compote in spring or poached apricot and cardamom come summer. In fall and winter, I bulk the oats up with cozy warming spices like cinnamon, ginger, and turmeric. Any time of year, you can infuse the oats with hibiscus, or sprinkle them with beautiful organic dried rose petals. The point is, anything goes once you nail the base. The oats are loaded with adaptogens, something we all need more of. Reishi mushrooms are immune-boosting and anxiety-easing. Ashwagandha powder balances stress levels and strengthens immunity. Lion's mane helps with mental clarity, and chaga fights free radicals and lowers inflammation. That adds up to a whole lot of goodness in your morning oats.

In a medium bowl, combine the oats and milk. Stir in the pistachios, dried fruit, sesame seeds, saffron, all 4 powders, maple syrup, and salt, mixing to combine.

Pack the mixture into a 1-quart (1 L) glass canning jar or other container and refrigerate overnight. The mushroom powders will infuse the nut milk and become stronger over time, and the oats will take on an earthy clay color.

Devour in the morning, topped with a pinch of saffron, a drizzle of maple syrup, fruit, nuts, and a sprinkle of mushroom powder.

RICE PORRIDGE WITH TROUT AND CRISPY MUSHROOMS

SERVES 2 OR 4

PORRIDGE

1 cup (205 g) sushi rice

10 cups (2.4 L) mushroom broth, such as Everyday Mushroom Broth (page 80) or Lion's Mane Broth (page 82)

One 8-ounce (225 g) trout or salmon fillet

2 tablespoons ghee

Himalayan pink salt

1 small bunch enoki mushrooms (3½ oz/100 g), trimmed to remove the base

FOR GARNISH

Spring garlic or thinly sliced scallions

Mushroom powder, any type

1 umeboshi plum, pitted and finely chopped, or ½ tablespoon umeboshi paste

Ume plum vinegar

A few pieces pickled ginger (I like turmeric-pickled ginger)

Pickled green coriander seeds

Mushroom Salt (page 53)

Bonito flakes

Years ago, I traveled to Japan's Isa Shima Peninsula, home to the famous ama divers. Tied to their baskets with rope, these free-diving fisherwomen plunge into the chilly water to gather fish and shellfish with nothing more than their hands. We struck up a conversation about katsuobushi, the magic, umami-rich dried tuna that, when shaved, becomes bonito flakes. They took us to meet a renowned katsuobushi maker nearby, who made us a bowl of overcooked rice porridge (okayu) with shavings of bonito that melted upon contact with the steamy rice. He told me that children are given okayu when they don't feel well. This sparked a memory of softly cooked, salty semolina with shavings of pecorino and butter, a dish my grandmother served me when I felt unwell. I realized every culture has its version of soft, feel-good porridge. This earthy variation, made with mushroom broth, is topped with Hudson Valley farm-raised trout, which has the pinkest flesh and lightest flavor, and enoki mushrooms; the long delicate stems crisp up so lyrically. This also makes a nice dinner for two.

Make the porridge: In a deep 5½-quart (5.2 L) heavy-bottomed pan (like a Dutch oven), combine the rice and 2 cups (480 ml) of the broth. Bring to a boil over medium-high heat. Reduce the heat to low and cook, gradually stirring in the remaining 8 cups (2 L) broth, until the rice has broken down, about 40 minutes. (If you need more liquid, add water.)

Meanwhile, cut the trout fillet into 2 or 4 thin strips, depending on serving size (1 strip per person). In a cast-iron skillet, heat 1 tablespoon of the ghee over medium-high heat until shimmering but not smoking. Add the trout strips, skin side down, and cook until the skin is super crispy, about 5 minutes. Avoid the temptation to flip it too soon; you want a crunchy crust to form. Sprinkle with pink salt. Flip and cook 5 minutes longer, sprinkling salt on the skin side.

In a large cast-iron or other skillet, heat the remaining 1 tablespoon ghee over medium heat. Add the enoki and cook until crisp, flipping with a spatula halfway through, about 5 minutes total.

Divide the porridge among serving bowls and top with trout and enoki. Add any desired garnishes, starting with spring garlic or scallions. Sprinkle with mushroom powder, a bit of chopped umeboshi, a dash of ume vinegar, the pickled ginger and green coriander seeds, mushroom salt, and a pinch of bonito flakes before serving.

COOKING WITH MUSHROOMS

SOFT SCRAMBLE WITH SHAVED TRUFFLE

SERVES 2

4 large eggs, preferably organic

2 tablespoons heavy cream

4 tablespoons (2 oz/60 g) salted
    butter, plus more for serving

Coarsely ground black pepper

1 small black truffle

Extra-virgin olive oil, for drizzling

Truffles, contrary to popular belief, are not meant to be saved for months, buried deep in rice at the back of your refrigerator as a way to preserve them. Rather, they should be put to deliciously good use right away! Serving soft scrambled eggs with truffle is a rich, decadent labor of love, a perfect breakfast for two on a weekend morning. If you are lucky enough to get your hands on a fresh truffle, make this recipe until there is no truffle left. (Otherwise, just sauté your favorite mushrooms with butter to top the soft scramble.) The creamy, buttery eggs do not come together quickly; be prepared to stand in front of your stove for up to 15 minutes. The key is whisking the eggs vigorously before adding them to the pan, and slowly bringing them up to temperature. Serve with Salty Sour Dark Rye (page 73) or Seedy Mushroom Crackers (page 69).

Crack the eggs into a large bowl and add the cream. Whisk vigorously until the whites, yolks, and cream are fully combined and smooth, about 1 minute.

On the lowest flame on your stovetop, heat a medium stainless steel, cast-iron, or nonstick skillet. Add the butter and heat until melted, then pour the eggs on top. Cook, stirring constantly with a flexible spatula or wooden spoon. The eggs will start to change in color as the butter is combined, from pale yellow to a richer yellow. Make sure to stir and scrape the bottom and sides of the pan. While it seems like nothing is happening, eventually the curds will begin to form. If no curds start to form after 10 minutes, increase the heat slightly. This process takes 10 to 15 minutes. Remove from the heat.

Garnish the eggs with a tiny pat of butter, pepper, a few shavings of truffle, and a tiny drizzle of oil. Serve immediately.

SOUPY EGGS WITH CHANTERELLES

SERVES 2

¼ cup (35 g) minced shallot (about
    1 medium)

2 teaspoons unseasoned rice
    vinegar or sherry vinegar

¼ cup (7 g) fresh flat-leaf parsley,
    coarsely chopped

1 thick slab of bread, preferably
    Salty Sour Dark Rye (page 73)

1 garlic clove, peeled

1 tablespoon unsalted butter

1 tablespoon extra-virgin olive oil

¼ pound (115 g) fresh chanterelles,
    such as yellow foot, trimmed
    and quartered

Coarse salt and cracked black
    pepper

2 large eggs

Flaky sea salt, such as Maldon, for
    finishing

Soupy soft eggs remind me of my paternal Grandfather Virgil, who ate them every morning for breakfast. These days, I gravitate toward this simple dish of soft runny eggs when feeling nostalgic. Here it gets an upgrade with seasonal chanterelles, thanks to the brilliant idea of my friend Frances. The chanterelles are so heavenly you might eat them all before they make it out of the pan. (Don't despair if you can't find fresh chanterelles; you can make the dish with any mushroom you enjoy eating.) Crunchy garlicky bread, combined with pickled shallots and parsley, nudges against the buttery mushrooms, and as soon as your spoon hits the bowl, the bread gets coated in the thick, warm yolk.

In a small bowl, toss the shallot with the vinegar and parsley to combine. Let sit (you want the shallot to quickly pickle while you finish the dish).

Toast the bread well. Remove and rub well with the garlic. Let the bread cool and chop it into large croutons or grate with a box grater if you prefer a finer crumb. Toss the crumbs into the shallot mixture.

In a small skillet, heat the butter and oil over medium-low heat. When the butter is foamy, add the chanterelles and season with coarse salt and pepper. Sauté until soft, about 4 minutes. Remove from the heat and let sit until ready to serve (or rewarm, if needed).

Set up a bowl of ice and water. Bring a small covered saucepan of water to a boil. Lower the eggs into the boiling water and boil for 5 minutes. Using a slotted spoon, immediately transfer to the ice bath for 30 seconds to stop the cooking.

Divide the mushrooms evenly between two serving bowls. Crack off the top one-third of each egg and gently scoop out directly over the mushrooms. Top with the bread crumb mixture, then finish with pepper and a little flaky salt before serving.

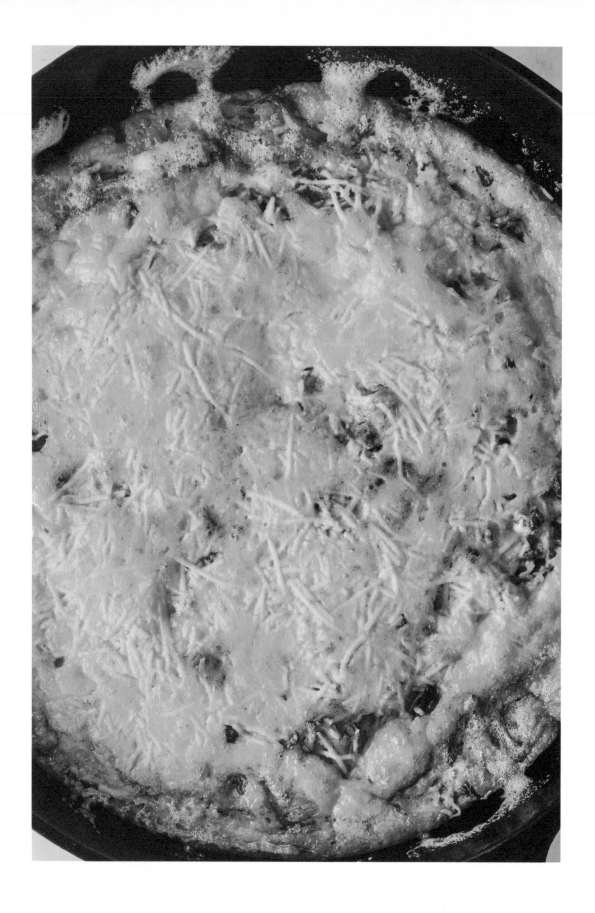

MUSHROOM FRITTATA

SERVES 6 TO 8

1 pound (455 g) fresh mushrooms,
    such as shiitake, oysters,
    maitake, or cremini
2 tablespoons unsalted butter
2 fresh oregano sprigs, leaves only
¼ cup (60 ml) extra-virgin olive oil
12 large eggs
1¼ cups (125 g) finely grated
    pecorino cheese
¼ teaspoon Himalayan pink salt
Finely grated zest and juice of
    ½ lemon, preferably organic
Fragrant fresh herbs, such as
    parsley, mint, and oregano,
    for garnish
Mushrooms à la Grecque (optional;
    page 65), for serving

My grandmother, an American-born Puglian, cooked in the manner of cucina povera, which she learned from her mother. This included a ton of vegetables, herbs, spicy dried chiles, and eggs. Frittatas made their way to our table for breakfast, lunch, and dinner, sometimes an herby one with oregano and mint, or a pile of leftover pasta, other times filled with slow-cooked, delightfully mushy broccoli rabe, and often a mushroom frittata, usually made with cremini. I like a combination of shiitake and maitake. The flavor is extraordinary—rich, earthy, and a little meaty without any heaviness. The key to this recipe, as with many Puglian dishes, is a nice amount of flavorful olive oil and some sharp, salty pecorino. You can top the frittata with the Mushrooms à la Grecque for a more substantial meal.

Preheat the oven to 450°F (230°C).

If using cremini or shiitake mushrooms, thinly slice with a mandoline or sharp knife. If using maitake or oyster, gently tear into small pieces.

In a 10-inch (25 cm) nonstick ovenproof lidded skillet, melt the butter over medium-low heat. When it starts to foam, add the mushrooms and oregano leaves and cook until soft and any liquid has been released, 3 to 5 minutes. Stir in the oil.

In a large bowl, whisk together the eggs, 1 cup (100 g) of the pecorino, and the salt.

Add the egg mixture to the pan and sprinkle the top with the remaining ¼ cup (25 g) cheese, the lemon zest, and lemon juice.

Reduce the heat to low, cover the pan, and cook until the bottom starts to brown, 5 to 10 minutes. (Check the eggs by lifting the bottom with a spatula.) Once the bottom starts to brown, transfer the pan to the oven, uncovered.

Bake for 5 minutes, then check to see if the top is puffing up. Cook a few minutes longer if not. The frittata is done when it starts to brown around the edges and a little bit on the top. Look for the oil bubbling up around the sides. This is totally normal. Once you remove the frittata from the oven to cool, the oil will get absorbed into the eggs, making it yummy and so delicious.

Serve the frittata warm or at room temperature, garnished with fresh herbs. If desired, top with mushrooms à la Grecque.

MORELS ON FRIED SOURDOUGH WITH SMASHED FAVAS AND PEAS

MAKES 6 PIECES

¼ cup (60 ml) plus 3 tablespoons extra-virgin olive oil, plus more for drizzling

6 thick-cut slices sourdough bread

Himalayan pink salt

1 garlic clove, peeled

1 cup (145 g) shelled fresh green peas (about 1 lb/455 g in the pods)

1 cup (150 g) shelled fresh fava beans (about 1 lb/455 g in the pods)

Finely grated zest and juice of 1 Meyer lemon, preferably organic

2 cups (3½ oz/100 g) cleaned and sliced morels (halve any smaller ones)

3-inch (8 cm) piece spring onion, thinly sliced

Fresh mint leaves, for garnish

Flowering herbs and edible flowers, for garnish (optional)

Flaky sea salt, such as Maldon, for finishing

After a long, spare winter of root vegetables and cold-storage fruits, it is nice to see my favorite spring ingredients reappear in the market. When morels, favas, and peas appear, I know that the new season is fully under way. Here I combined the three with garlicky fried bread for a perfect lazy weekend breakfast. The smashed peas are a fresh ode to English mushy peas. To clean morels, cut them in half and brush out their hollow stems to get rid of any dirt or critters. Make sure to cook the mushrooms all the way through, as they can be toxic when raw.

In a large cast-iron skillet, heat 2 tablespoons of the oil over medium heat. Arrange the sourdough to fit snugly in the pan. Fry the bread until browned on both sides, adding more oil if needed and sprinkling both sides with pink salt. Remove the bread from the skillet and rub both sides of each slice with the garlic clove. Set aside to cool.

Set up a bowl of ice and water. Bring a small pot of salted water to a boil. Blanch the peas for 30 to 45 seconds, then transfer to the ice bath with a slotted spoon. Drain the peas and transfer to a large bowl. Blanch and cool the favas, then peel them (see Note) and add them to the bowl.

Add the ¼ cup (60 ml) oil and ¼ teaspoon pink salt to the peas and favas and toss to coat. With a potato masher, smash the favas and peas to a chunky texture. Add the lemon zest and half the juice.

In the same cast-iron skillet, heat the remaining 1 tablespoon oil over medium heat. Add the morels and spring onion and sauté until soft, 3 to 5 minutes.

Arrange the fried bread on a platter. Spoon the smashed favas and peas onto each piece and top with morels. Garnish with mint. If desired, also garnish with flowering herbs and flowers. Drizzle with the remaining lemon juice and a generous drizzle of oil. Sprinkle with flaky salt.

Note: After blanching and then cooling the favas in the ice bath, peel the beans by hand. It may seem laborious at first, but it's quite meditative, and you will get the hang of it. Pretty soon, the tough little skins will pop right off.

COOKING WITH MUSHROOMS

MUSHROOM RÖSTI WITH HERBY SALAD

SERVES 4

RÖSTI

2 pounds (910 g) German Butterball
  or Yukon Gold potatoes
1 tablespoon plus a pinch of
  Himalayan pink salt
½ pound (225 g) mixed fresh
  shiitake and oyster mushrooms
1 cup (40 g) coarsely chopped fresh
  herbs, such as mint, oregano,
  and chives
1 tablespoon salted capers, rinsed
  and patted dry
1 garlic clove, finely grated with
  a Microplane
½ teaspoon coarsely ground black
  pepper
4 tablespoons ghee
2 tablespoons extra-virgin olive oil

HERBY SALAD

½ cup (15 g) torn fresh herbs, such
  as mint, oregano, and chives
Flaky sea salt, such as Maldon
Finely grated zest and juice of
  ½ lemon, preferably organic
Coarsely ground black pepper

As a child growing up on a farm, my weekends meant early-morning chores. I am talking up at 5:30 a.m. to milk and feed our two Jersey cows, collect eggs, and often make butter before breakfast. The kitchen table was a mass of crispy fried eggs, custardy scramble with the yellowest yolks, potatoes (usually a big rösti or hash), butter and thick cream, and hot chocolate. Here I have adapted a rösti to include shiitakes and oyster mushrooms and a ton of herbs cooked in umami-rich ghee.

Make the rösti: Wash and peel the potatoes. Using the largest holes of a box grater, shred the potatoes into a large bowl. Add 1 tablespoon of the pink salt and mix again. Let sit for 10 to 15 minutes to release liquid.

Working in batches, squeeze excess liquid from the potato mixture and transfer to a dry bowl. Repeat the process three times, discarding the liquid and transferring to a dry bowl.

Stem the shiitakes and thinly slice the caps; coarsely chop the oyster mushrooms. Place the mushrooms in a bowl (reserve the stems for stock) and add the chopped herbs, capers, grated garlic, a pinch of pink salt, and the pepper. Toss to combine and let sit for 15 minutes. Squeeze out any liquid (sometimes mushrooms will release a ton of water, sometimes none at all).

Combine the mushrooms with the potatoes, using your hands to mix thoroughly. Let the mixture sit for 10 minutes; repeat the water-squeezing process once or twice, until there is no liquid left.

In a nonstick medium skillet, heat 2 tablespoons of the ghee and 1 tablespoon of the oil over medium-low heat until shimmering. Add the potato-mushroom mixture and press into an even layer. Cover and cook until the underside is nicely browned, 15 to 20 minutes (you are steaming the mushrooms and potatoes while crisping the bottom). Turn the pan intermittently to keep the cooking even. When the bottom is crisp, invert the rösti onto a plate. Add the remaining 2 tablespoons ghee and 1 tablespoon oil to the skillet and slide the rösti back into it, uncooked side down. Cook over medium-low heat, turning the pan to cook evenly, until the underside is browned and crisp, 15 to 20 minutes. It should be the color of almost burnt toast. The mushrooms will get darker than the potatoes as they caramelize. Slide the rösti onto a plate for serving.

Make the herby salad: Toss the torn herbs with a little flaky salt, the lemon zest, a squeeze of lemon juice, and some black pepper.

Top the rösti with the salad and serve.

4

MIDDAY MUSHROOMS

MUSHROOM CEVICHE TOSTADAS

SERVES 4 TO 6 GENEROUSLY

1 tablespoon extra-virgin olive oil, plus more for drizzling

7 ounces (200 g) white or brown beech (Bunapi) mushrooms, trimmed

½ teaspoon Himalayan pink salt, plus more to taste

½ large red onion, thinly sliced into half-moons

Juice of 4 limes (about ⅓ cup/ 80 ml)

2 Meyer lemons, 1 zested and juiced, 1 zested and supremed (see Note)

1 teaspoon dark brown sugar

¼ jalapeño, seeded and finely chopped (optional)

⅓ cup (10 g) fresh mint leaves, gently torn

⅓ cup (10 g) fresh cilantro leaves, gently torn

1 tablespoon fresh oregano leaves (about 2 sprigs)

⅓ cup (35 g) salted capers, rinsed well and patted dry

¼ teaspoon Aleppo pepper

⅓ cup (30 g) very thinly sliced celery (use a mandoline if you have one)

1 large avocado, cubed

Flaky sea salt, such as Maldon

One 1-pound (455 g) package tostadas

This recipe is inspired by two of my most memorable meals—the tuna tostada at Contramar, Gabriela Cámara's famous all-day seafood café in Mexico City, and Gastón Acurio's ceviche in the seaside city of Lima, on the edge of the Pacific Ocean in Peru. When I started developing this book, I thought of all the flavors I like to eat, and then I started to imagine how mushrooms could work with them. That is how I came to the mushroom ceviche on a crisp, crunchy tostada. I chose Bunapi (white beech) mushrooms and left them whole because they look pretty and the chew mimics that of squid, but you can chop them up a little if you'd prefer. While the fish in ceviche is generally uncooked and cured in citrus juice, I cook the mushrooms briefly to soften them and allow them to absorb the flavors of lime, onion, chile, and herbs more quickly. Once the flavors have melded, add a handful of fresh herbs. This dish is an ode to both Lima and Mexico City, and to the two chefs who continue to inspire me.

In a cast-iron skillet or small Dutch oven, heat the oil over medium-low heat. Add the mushrooms and ¼ teaspoon of the pink salt and cook, stirring constantly, until they release their juices, 3 to 5 minutes (they should still retain their form). Remove from the heat and set aside.

Place the onion slices in a large bowl. Add the lime juice, lemon zest, lemon juice, lemon segments, sugar, and remaining ¼ teaspoon pink salt, tossing to coat. Add the jalapeño, if using. Cover and let sit for at least 10 minutes to cure the onions.

Add the mint, cilantro, oregano, capers, Aleppo pepper, celery, and mushrooms, gently tossing to combine. Let sit for another 15 minutes. Gently toss in the avocado just before serving. Add pink salt to taste (the capers are salty so you may not need any). Finish with a drizzle of oil and some flaky salt.

Serve the ceviche on the tostadas.

Note: To supreme lemons (or any citrus fruit), start by trimming the ends with a very sharp knife. Set one of the flat ends on a cutting board and remove the peel by following the curve of the fruit. Next, working from the outside toward the center, slice the fruit into sections, cutting as close to the membranes as you can and taking care to keep the segments intact. Transfer the segments to a bowl as you work, and then squeeze the membranes over the bowl to capture the juice.

COOKING WITH MUSHROOMS

MUSHROOM LARB

SERVES 4

SAUCE

Finely grated zest and juice of
    8 limes, preferably organic
    (⅔ to 1 cup/160 to 240 ml juice)
2 tablespoons fish sauce
2 tablespoons maple syrup
2 tablespoons light brown sugar
2 garlic cloves, finely grated with
    a Microplane
2-inch (5 cm) nub fresh ginger,
    peeled and finely grated with
    a Microplane
1 teaspoon chili-garlic sauce

LARB

¼ cup (60 ml) plus 2 tablespoons
    olive oil
2 pounds (910 g) fresh cremini
    mushrooms, trimmed and very
    finely chopped to resemble
    ground meat
2 small shallots, minced
4 makrut lime leaves, finely
    chopped
2-inch (5 cm) piece lemongrass,
    thinly sliced
2 garlic cloves, finely grated with
    a Microplane
2 tablespoons fish sauce

FOR SERVING

6 heads Little Gem lettuce or
    1 large head Bibb lettuce
Fresh mint and cilantro
Lime wedges
Chives (optional)
Scallions (optional)

Larb hits the sour, salty, sweet, and spicy notes that are so specific to Southeast Asia. The dish is most often made with ground meat, but I replaced the protein with mushrooms and amped up the sweet-salty flavors. I prefer to chop the mushrooms by hand with a knife, rather than buzzing them in a food processor, to keep the sizes a bit irregular, but use a food processor if you want. Just be sure to pulse, not process, to avoid overdoing it and turning the mushrooms to mush. Because they release a lot of water as they cook, the mushrooms are crisped in a hot oven after they're sautéed. Served in icy, crunchy lettuce leaves, the larb feels light as a feather but still packs a serious flavor punch.

Preheat the oven to 475°F (245°C).

Make the sauce: In a small bowl, combine all the ingredients and set aside to let the flavors meld.

Make the larb: In a large heavy-bottomed pot, heat ¼ cup (60 ml) of the oil over medium-low heat until warm. Add the mushrooms, shallots, lime leaves, lemongrass, and garlic. Sauté for about 5 minutes, then stir in the fish sauce and continue cooking until the mushrooms are beginning to brown, about 5 minutes longer.

Since the mushrooms release a lot of water, you want to crisp them in the oven. Drizzle the remaining 2 tablespoons oil on a large sheet pan, add the mushroom mixture, and toss. Spread into an even layer and roast until the moisture has evaporated and the mushrooms are crisp, about 30 minutes, stirring every 10 minutes or so.

While the mushrooms are in the oven, prepare the lettuce: Remove the cores and any tough outer leaves (you want the tender inner leaves). Wash the leaves and place them in an ice water bath so they remain crisp. Just before serving, lay the pieces of lettuce out to dry and gently pat with a paper towel to remove excess water.

Dividing evenly, spoon the mushrooms into lettuce leaves. Arrange the leaves on a platter, spoon some sauce over each, and serve with mint, cilantro, lime wedges, and any optional accompaniments.

HEALING CHICKEN BROTH WITH MUSHROOMS, OREGANO, AND MINT

MAKES 4 QUARTS (3.8 L)

1 whole chicken (2½ to 3 lb/1.1 to 1.4 kg), preferably organic

2-inch (5 cm) nub fresh ginger, finely grated with a Microplane

1 large yellow onion or 2 shallots, coarsely chopped

10 garlic cloves, smashed and peeled

¼ dried red chile, such as chile de árbol, crumbled (optional)

1 tablespoon Himalayan pink salt, plus more to taste

6 sprigs each mixed fresh herbs: oregano, mint, and cilantro, tied into a bundle, plus more of each, for garnish

5 quarts (4.7 L) water

½ pound (225 g) fresh shiitake mushrooms, thinly sliced

3 limes, for serving

Extra-virgin olive oil, for serving

This vibrant soup, inspired by a broth I had in Oaxaca, Mexico, tastes light and fresh thanks to an abundance of herbs, garlic, and ginger. At the Sunday-morning market in Tlacolula, we found ourselves at the stall of a woman selling bowls of chicken broth, ladled from a giant bubbling pot and topped with chopped white onion and jalapeño; the chicken was added separately by request. The broth is nothing like the bone broth I make every week with the carcass of a roast chicken. Instead, it is the palest yellow-green, taking color and flavor from the essential oils in the herbs.

My grandmother made a similar soup with diced zucchini (cooked until soft), fresh oregano, mint, and white onion; she topped each bowl with a shower of pecorino. Here I include a crushed red chile for a little heat and cook sliced shiitakes in the broth before serving. The broth is also nice on its own as a healing, feel-good elixir when you are under the weather.

Place the chicken in an 8- to 12-quart (7.6 to 11.3 L) stockpot. Add the ginger, onion, garlic, crumbled chile (if using), salt, herb bundle, and water. Bring to a gentle simmer (not a rapid boil) over medium-low heat. Continue to simmer gently until the chicken is cooked through, 45 minutes to 1 hour.

Discard the herb bundle. Transfer the chicken to a colander set over a bowl and let cool in the sink, 15 to 20 minutes.

When the chicken is cool enough to handle, discard the skin. With a knife or with your fingertips, remove the breasts of the bird and all the other meat and set it aside. (Discard the bones or freeze them to use for stock at a later time.) Shred the chicken and return it to the broth in the pot.

Add the sliced shiitakes and return the broth to a simmer over low heat. Simmer until the mushrooms are cooked, about 15 minutes.

Season the soup with salt to taste and ladle into bowls for serving. Top with fresh herbs, a squeeze of lime, and a drizzle of oil.

If not serving immediately, let the soup cool completely, then transfer to glass jars for storage. Refrigerate for up to 5 days or freeze for up to 6 months (if freezing, leave ¾ inch/2 cm of free space at the top of the jar for expansion).

COOKING WITH MUSHROOMS

BROWN BUTTER PUFF PASTRY CROSTATA WITH ANCHOVY AND 'SHROOMS

SERVES 8 TO 10

4 tablespoons (2 oz/60 g) salted butter
1 teaspoon coriander seeds
¼ teaspoon chile flakes or 1 dried red chile de árbol, crushed
1 medium shallot, thinly sliced
6 white anchovies (boquerones)
¾ pound (340 g) mixed fresh mushrooms, trimmed and torn or sliced if large
¼ cup (60 ml) dry white or orange wine
2 teaspoons ume plum vinegar
1 cup (50 g) torn mixed fresh herbs, such as lovage, garlic chives, and oregano, plus a few sprigs for topping
1 leek, thinly sliced and well washed
Pinch of Himalayan pink salt
⅛ teaspoon coarsely ground black pepper
One 14-ounce (395 g) package all-butter frozen puff pastry, such as Dufour
All-purpose flour, for rolling out pastry
1 cup (3½ oz/100 g) coarsely grated Gruyère cheese
Finely grated zest of 1 lemon, preferably organic
1 large egg yolk
Flaky sea salt, such as Maldon

While I love to make homemade crostata dough, this recipe came about when friends popped by unexpectedly and I had frozen puff pastry on hand. It comes together quickly for an impromptu aperitivo or weekend brunch. You can use a mix of mushrooms here; any variety would work. I like a combination of chanterelle, oyster, black trumpet, maitake, and matsutake. For a beautiful finish, reserve a few especially nice-looking mushrooms from the bunch and sauté them in about 2 tablespoons of butter until glossy, then arrange them atop the baked crostata just before serving. Serve with a bright, herby salad and chilled orange wine.

Preheat the oven to 450°F (230°C).

In a large skillet, heat the butter over medium heat until foamy and just beginning to brown. Stir in the coriander seeds and chile flakes. Add the shallot and anchovies and cook until the anchovies begin to melt and the shallot becomes translucent. Add the mushrooms and cook until they soften, 3 to 4 minutes. Add the wine and vinegar and cook until absorbed. Reduce the heat to low and add the herbs, leek, pink salt, and pepper.

Remove from the heat and set aside to cool.

Gently unwrap the frozen puff pastry. If the pastry is too hard and the pieces start to come apart, let it rest at room temperature for 10 minutes or so.

Place a piece of parchment on a work surface and lightly flour it. Gently roll the pastry just once or twice to soften any seams, then gently roll it into a 12 × 14-inch (30 × 35 cm) rectangle. Transfer the parchment and pastry to a large baking sheet. Sprinkle with half the Gruyère, leaving a 1-inch (3 cm) border on all sides. Top with the mushroom filling. Top the mushrooms with the lemon zest. Add the remaining cheese to cover the filling, top with an oregano sprig or two, and fold the edges over to make a border.

In a small bowl, whisk the egg yolk, then brush the edges of the pastry with it. Sprinkle the pastry with a little flaky salt.

Bake until the crostata is golden brown and crisp, 20 to 25 minutes. Sprinkle with a little more flaky salt and serve warm.

CRISPY SHIITAKE "BACON" ENDIVE WEDGE SALAD

SERVES 4

4 large or 6 medium shiitake mushrooms, trimmed and very thinly sliced

1 tablespoon extra-virgin olive oil, plus more for drizzling

1 tablespoon dark soy sauce

2 tablespoons maple syrup

½ teaspoon Miso Mushroom Paste (page 57)

1 tablespoon unseasoned rice vinegar

½ teaspoon cracked black pepper, plus more for serving

4 large endives

1 large head radicchio

⅓ cup (2¼ oz/65 g) blue cheese, such as Bayley Hazen or Danish, crumbled into chunks, plus more (optional) for garnish

1 cup (225 g) whole-milk yogurt or sour cream (or buttermilk, for a thinner dressing)

Finely grated zest and juice of 1 Meyer lemon, preferably organic

1 garlic clove, finely grated with a Microplane

Flaky sea salt, such as Maldon

Whenever I see a wedge salad on the menu, I have to order it. One of my first work trips after the world began to open up again post-pandemic lockdown was to Chicago. We stayed downtown, across from a steakhouse that has been there since the 1920s. Their wedge salad did not disappoint. The cold, crunchy iceberg got me thinking about using chicories in its place. To me, it's really all about that crunch. I love bitter flavors, and chicories—which include the radicchio and endive here—are both bitter and extremely beautiful. The rich dressing here pairs perfectly with the almost fatty shiitakes as they take on the character of crisp, maple-cured bacon.

Preheat the oven to 375°F (190°C).

In a large bowl, combine the shiitakes, oil, soy sauce, maple syrup, miso mushroom paste, vinegar, and pepper. Set aside to marinate for 30 minutes while the oven preheats.

Arrange the mushrooms in a single layer on a baking sheet. Roast for 20 minutes, flipping halfway through.

Meanwhile, trim the endives and halve lengthwise. Quarter the radicchio. Place the radicchio and endives on a serving plate or platter.

In a small bowl, stir to combine the blue cheese, yogurt, lemon zest, lemon juice, and garlic, leaving a few big pieces of cheese.

To assemble the salad, drizzle the dressing generously over the radicchio and endive. Top with the shiitake "bacon," a little cracked pepper, flaky salt, and a drizzle of oil. If desired, garnish with more blue cheese.

COOKING WITH MUSHROOMS

MUSHROOM MINT SUMMER ROLLS

MAKES 12 ROLLS

One 8-ounce (225 g) package
    enoki mushrooms, trimmed
One 8-ounce (225 g) package
    brown beech mushrooms,
    trimmed
1½ teaspoons Himalayan pink salt
1½ cups (360 ml) unseasoned rice
    vinegar
½ cup (120 ml) water
3 tablespoons maple syrup
2 teaspoons honey
1 teaspoon coriander seeds,
    crushed with the side of a knife
¼ dried red chile, such as chile de
    árbol, or 1 teaspoon chile flakes
4 ounces (115 g) rice vermicelli
Twelve 9-inch (23 cm) spring roll
    wrappers
1 cup (36 g) edible flowers, such
    as organic, pesticide-free
    roses, marigolds, and calendula
    (optional)
1 cup (30 g) torn mint leaves
1 cup (1½ oz/40 g) sprouts, such as
    radish or pea
Green Goddess Dressing (page 85),
    for serving

A wander through the farmers' market lends endless inspiration for making summer rolls. The summer roll is a blank canvas; my only constant is to add something pickled, something crunchy, and loads of mint. I pick up edible flowers, sprouts and shoots, and seasonal vegetables. Here I use mild enoki and brown beech mushrooms. Pickled in a sweet-and-sour brine, they take on a soft, almost vermicelli-like texture. You can pickle other vegetables, like radishes and carrots, along with the mushrooms; the brine is super versatile. Place the flowers down on each softened spring roll wrapper first so they will show through once you roll it up.

On a baking sheet lined with parchment, lay out the mushrooms. Sprinkle with the salt and gently toss to coat completely. Set the mushrooms aside for 30 minutes to release water.

In a nonreactive medium saucepan, combine the vinegar, water, maple syrup, honey, coriander seeds, and chile. Bring to a simmer over medium-low heat. Add the mushrooms and cook at a bare simmer, 3 to 5 minutes. Remove the pot from the heat and let the mushrooms cool in the pickling liquid.

Cook the vermicelli noodles according to the package directions and set aside.

To assemble the rolls, partially fill a shallow medium bowl with warm water. One at a time, dip a spring roll wrapper until just softened, but not mushy and falling apart. Carefully remove from the water bath and place on a large plate or work surface.

On a clean tea towel, lay out the wrapper. Dividing evenly, place a layer of edible flowers (if using) in the center, then top with some vermicelli noodles. Add pickled mushrooms, mint leaves, and sprouts. Fold the left and right sides over the filling, and then fold up from the bottom and roll tightly away from you until the filling is all tucked in and enclosed. Set the summer roll on a plate, seam side down, and repeat with the remaining wrappers and fillings to make more rolls. Serve with the dressing.

MUSHROOM TACOS THREE WAYS

SERVES 8 TO 10

**MUSHROOM TACO FILLINGS
(PICK ONE OR ALL)**
**Mushroom and Cauliflower
    Carnitas (page 135)**
**Lion's Mane with Spruce Salt and
    Spring Garlic (page 136)**
**Maitake with Preserved Lemon and
    Ume Plum Vinegar (page 139)**

FOR SERVING
Corn tortillas, warmed
Cilantro Mint Crema (page 86)
Juniper-Pickled Onions (page 93)
Lime wedges

*Often when we gather in a large group to celebrate one thing or
another, we make tacos. I usually slow-cook a pork shoulder to satisfy
the carnivores of the group. Lately, more and more mushrooms have
been taking center stage at these gatherings. Roasting, whether
quick or slow, coaxes all the woodsy, earthy, umami flavors from the
mushrooms; they become something else entirely when combined
with aromatic spices, herbs, and citrus notes. You have three
choices of fillings here. Make any or all of them, and then set out the
accompaniments: warm tortillas, pickled onions, cilantro crema, and
lime wedges for squeezing.*

Make the filling(s) of choice. Set out the filling(s), warmed tortillas,
crema, pickled onions, and lime wedges for squeezing.

Mushroom and Cauliflower Carnitas

SERVES 10 TO 12

2 medium heads cauliflower (about
   2 lb/910 g total)
2 pounds (910 g) fresh oyster
   mushrooms, trimmed and
   gently torn
4 tablespoons (50 g) ghee or
   unsalted butter, 2 tablespoons
   melted, 2 tablespoons at room
   temperature
¾ cup (180 ml) fresh lime juice
   (from 6 to 8 limes)
1 large dried red chile, such as
   chile de árbol, crumbled, or
   ½ teaspoon chile flakes
2 tablespoons extra-virgin olive oil
¼ teaspoon Himalayan pink salt
¼ teaspoon coarsely ground black
   pepper
3 tablespoons maple syrup
¼ cup (60 ml) fish sauce
9 garlic cloves, 2 finely grated
   with a Microplane, 7 smashed
   and peeled
1 teaspoon ground turmeric or
   Miso Powder (page 53)

These carnitas are one of my staple taco fillings, inspired by a spectacular Brussels sprout taco at Atla in New York. You can enjoy the mushrooms and cauliflower right out of the oven, when they are quite soft and juicy, or roast them on a sheet pan a bit longer until crisp and crunchy. (You can also easily halve the recipe.)

Preheat the oven to 300°F (150°C).

Turn the cauliflower heads upside down and carve out most of the central cores without cutting into the florets. Set aside.

Place the torn mushrooms in the bottom of a 10-quart (9.5 L) Dutch oven or two smaller ovenproof pots.

In a small bowl, whisk together the melted ghee, lime juice, chile, oil, salt, pepper, maple syrup, fish sauce, and both the grated and smashed garlic. The sauce will be thick and glossy.

Spoon half the sauce over the mushrooms. Place the cauliflower on top. Rub the room-temperature ghee all over the heads of cauliflower, then spoon the remaining sauce over the cauliflower. With a small fine-mesh sieve, dust the cauliflower with the turmeric.

Transfer the pot to the oven. Roast until the cauliflower heads are soft, 2 to 2½ hours, basting with juices halfway through.

Remove the pot from the oven and transfer the cauliflower to a cutting board. Reserve the sauce at the bottom of the pot. Coarsely chop the cauliflower into small pieces. If you would like crispy carnitas, increase the oven temperature to 425°F (220°C) and place a large sheet pan in the oven to heat up. Toss the mushrooms and chopped cauliflower on the hot sheet pan, transfer to the oven, and roast until crisp, 15 to 20 minutes.

To serve, pour the reserved sauce over the cauliflower and mushrooms.

Lion's Mane with Spruce Salt and Spring Garlic

SERVES 4

2 pounds (455 g) fresh lion's mane mushrooms, left whole or broken into smallish clusters

6 tablespoons (3 oz/85 g) unsalted butter, cut into ½-inch (1 cm) pieces

1 teaspoon spruce tip salt

1 teaspoon cracked black pepper

1 stalk of spring garlic, thinly sliced, or ½ large shallot, thinly sliced

¼ cup (5 g) dried leeks (see page 41)

Juice of 1 lemon

1 teaspoon ume plum vinegar, for drizzling

Himalayan pink salt

When I roast the lion's mane for this taco filling, I like to sprinkle them with some type of homemade specialty salt—in this case, a fruity, floral spruce salt with a hit of piney resin—and a few aromatics like spring garlic and dried leeks. I make spruce salt every spring when the vibrant green tips come into season. Use any type of specialty salt you have; yuzu, ramp, and leek salt are all good choices here. In addition to (or in place of) the toppings listed in Mushroom Tacos Three Ways (page 132), serve with chopped white onion and cilantro leaves.

Preheat the oven to 425°F (220°C).

In a Dutch oven or on a large sheet pan, arrange the mushrooms in an even layer and tuck in the pats of butter evenly throughout. Scatter the spruce tip salt and pepper over the top and sprinkle with the sliced spring garlic and dried leeks. Drizzle with the lemon juice and vinegar.

Roast for 15 to 20 minutes. Toss the mushrooms with the pan juices and roast until the edges are crispy and brown, about 15 minutes longer. Remove the mushrooms from the oven and transfer to a cutting board. Using two forks, shred the mushrooms into small pieces. Transfer the pieces to 1 large or 2 medium cast-iron skillets and cook on the stovetop over medium heat until nicely crisped all over, 5 to 10 minutes.

Season with pink salt to taste.

COOKING WITH MUSHROOMS

Maitake with Preserved Lemon and Ume Plum Vinegar

SERVES 4

1 pound (455 g) fresh maitake
mushrooms, gently shredded
into smaller pieces

3 tablespoons extra-virgin olive oil

¼ preserved lemon, store-bought
or homemade (page 94), seeded
and cut into tiny pieces

1 teaspoon nettle powder
(optional)

1 teaspoon ume plum vinegar

Cracked black pepper

Himalayan pink salt

This taco filling is nicely salty and a tiny bit briny from the preserved lemon. I also like the grassy notes that the nettle powder brings to the woody maitake mushrooms, but it's optional. The recipe doubles easily if you're planning to make more tacos.

Preheat the oven to 400°F (200°C).

Place the mushroom pieces in a large cast-iron skillet or on a sheet pan. Drizzle with the oil, then toss with the preserved lemon. Sprinkle with the nettle powder (if using) and drizzle with the vinegar. Season with a few turns of pepper.

Roast for 20 minutes, tossing halfway through. Season with salt to taste before serving.

SHIITAKE KOFTA

SERVES 4 TO 6

SPICE MIX

1 tablespoon coriander seeds

¼ teaspoon black peppercorns

2 teaspoons cumin seeds

2 teaspoons fennel seeds

½ teaspoon Himalayan pink salt

½ teaspoon ground Kashmiri chile

½ teaspoon paprika

¼ teaspoon ground cinnamon

¼ teaspoon ground cloves

⅛ teaspoon freshly grated nutmeg

KOFTA

1 pound (455 g) fresh shiitake
    mushrooms, minced

1 cup (40 g) chopped fresh cilantro
    (about 1 small bunch)

1 small shallot, minced

2 garlic cloves, minced

1-inch (3 cm) nub fresh ginger,
    peeled and grated

1 teaspoon red miso paste or Miso
    Mushroom Paste (page 57)

½ cup (45 g) chickpea flour

2 large eggs

1 tablespoon extra-virgin olive oil
    or ghee

½ teaspoon honey

½ teaspoon Himalayan pink salt

FOR FRYING

Chickpea flour, for dredging

2 tablespoons extra-virgin olive oil
    or ghee

Coarse salt and freshly ground
    black pepper

Kofta is a Middle Eastern and South Asian dish traditionally made of minced meat and spices formed into patties and cooked on skewers. Here I replaced the meat with minced shiitakes and amped up the spices, garlic, and cilantro for an earthy vegetarian version. You can combine all the kofta ingredients and chill the mixture in the refrigerator for up to a day before cooking to allow more time for the flavors to develop. Serve stuffed into warm toasted pitas with pickled vegetables, hummus, shaved radish, and the Double-Cumin Yogurt Dip (page 90).

Make the spice mix: In a dry cast-iron skillet over medium-low heat, toast the coriander seeds, peppercorns, cumin seeds, and fennel seeds until fragrant, 2 to 3 minutes, tossing and watching closely so they don't burn. Remove from the pan and let the spices cool, then crush them with a mortar and pestle or with the side of a chef's knife. Stir in the pink salt, chile, paprika, cinnamon, cloves, and nutmeg.

Make the kofta: In a large bowl, combine the spice mix, shiitakes, cilantro, shallot, garlic, ginger, miso, chickpea flour, eggs, oil, honey, and pink salt. Cover and refrigerate to firm up for 1 hour or up to 1 day.

Fry the kofta: Form the mixture into 1½- to 2-inch (4 to 5 cm) rounds (you should get 12 to 15) and set on a baking sheet. Press into small patties, taking care not to flatten them. You want them to remain rounded and relatively small; if they're too flat, they will break apart and crumble. Gently dip both sides of each patty in chickpea flour.

In a cast-iron or nonstick skillet, heat the oil over medium-low heat until it shimmers. Working in batches if needed, fry the patties until the undersides are crisp, 3 to 5 minutes. Flip and fry on the other side for another 3 to 5 minutes. Transfer to a wire rack or paper towels to drain, and season with coarse salt and pepper before serving.

COOKING WITH MUSHROOMS

GRILLED CHEESE WITH MUSHROOM-OLIVE-PEPPERONCINI RELISH

MAKES 4 SANDWICHES

RELISH
½ pound (225 g) fresh mushrooms (I like maitake and oyster here), trimmed and finely chopped
¼ cup (30 g) finely chopped stemmed pepperoncini (6 or 7 small)
¼ cup (30 g) finely chopped pitted Castelvetrano olives
Finely grated zest and juice of ½ lemon

SANDWICHES
1 loaf sourdough miche, pain de mie, or Pullman bread
One 8-ounce (225 g) block extra-sharp cheddar cheese
4 tablespoons (2 oz/60 g) unsalted butter, at room temperature
Flaky sea salt, such as Maldon

A grilled cheese should be perfectly crunchy on the outside and soft and gooey on the inside. This one, a grown-up version of my favorite childhood sandwich, is inspired by both an Italian antipasto plate and the English cheese toastie, with its sweet-and-sour Branston pickle. First, I make a relish by dry sautéing mushrooms (they keep a bit more freshness than when cooked in butter or oil), chopped pepperoncini, Castelvetrano olives, and a hit of citrus. Then, I sandwich it with thin shavings of extra-sharp cheddar between thick slices of sourdough miche. The fattiness of the cheese and the earthiness of the mushroom pair perfectly with the spicy peppers and salty olives. The relish is a star on its own—try it stirred into labneh as a dip or spooned alongside grilled fish or on top of roasted vegetables. Serve the sandwiches with a side of Mushrooms à la Grecque (page 65), if desired.

Make the relish: Heat a cast-iron skillet over medium-low heat. Add the chopped mushrooms and dry sauté for about 4 minutes, stirring constantly to prevent sticking (they will release moisture as they cook).

In a bowl, combine the mushrooms, pepperoncini, olives, lemon zest, and lemon juice.

Make the sandwiches: Cut eight ½-inch-thick (1 cm) slices of bread. Using a mandoline or a very sharp knife, shave the cheese into very thin slices. Place the bread on a cutting board or sheet pan and spread ½ tablespoon butter on one side of each slice. Flip 4 slices over, buttered side down, and top each with 4 tablespoons relish, followed by cheese slices, dividing evenly. Top with the remaining 4 slices of bread, buttered side up.

Heat a cast-iron skillet over medium heat. Cook the sandwiches until golden, about 4 minutes per side, pressing down firmly on each side with a spatula occasionally, and flipping and pressing at least twice. Sprinkle both sides of each sandwich with salt. Serve hot.

SALAD OF PINK RADICCHIOS, CITRUS, AND MUSHROOM BAGNA CAUDA

SERVES 4 TO 6

3 Cara Cara oranges or satsuma
    mandarins
1 large head pink radicchio (also
    known as La Rosa del Veneto),
    trimmed, washed, and gently
    patted dry
1 large head Castelfranco
    radicchio, trimmed, washed,
    and gently patted dry
2 shallots, thinly sliced
¼ cup (60 ml) sherry vinegar
1 teaspoon honey
½ teaspoon Himalayan pink salt
2 ounces (60 g) parmesan cheese
½ teaspoon flaky sea salt, such as
    Maldon, plus more to taste
Cracked black pepper
2 tablespoons Brown Butter
    Porcini Bagna Cauda (page 150),
    warmed
Extra-virgin olive oil (preferably a
    grassy, spicy one), for drizzling

I don't know which I love more in late winter, the beautiful varieties of hot-pink and blush-colored radicchios that arrive in the market or the vibrant array of seasonal citrus. Here I combined the two with the earthy, buttery Brown Butter Porcini Bagna Cauda I developed for cocktail hour to create a sweet, bitter, salty, smoky salad. The nuttiness of the parmesan tempers the acidity of the citrus and mellows the shallot. The recipe serves 4 to 6 but you may just find yourself digging in with both hands and not sharing, as I have been known to do!

Juice 1 orange to get ¼ cup (60 ml). Using a sharp knife, carefully cut the peel off the remaining 2 oranges, following the curve of the fruit and removing as little flesh as possible. Slice the peeled oranges crosswise into ½-inch-thick (1 cm) rounds.

Place the radicchio leaves in a large serving bowl.

In a small bowl, stir to combine the shallots, vinegar, honey, orange juice, and pink salt. Set aside to let the shallots mellow.

On the thinnest setting of a mandoline (or with a very sharp knife), shave the Parmigiano.

Pour the shallot-citrus mixture over the radicchio leaves and toss thoroughly with your hands. Add the orange rounds, flaky salt, and pepper to taste and toss again.

Drizzle the warmed bagna cauda over the salad. Top with the shaved cheese, a little more cracked pepper, and a drizzle of oil just before serving.

COOKING WITH MUSHROOMS

MAITAKE RAMEN

SERVES 4

DASHI
2 pieces kombu (dried kelp), 3 ×
    4 inches (8 × 10 cm) each
¼ cup (1 oz/20 g) dried maitakes
¼ cup (¼ oz/8 g) dried wood ears
4 dried shiitakes (about 20 g)
4 cups (1 L) just-boiled water

RAMEN BASE SEED BUTTER
½ cup 'Shroomy Nut and Seed
    Butter (page 61; without maple
    syrup) or store-bought nut
    butter
1 cup (140 g) sunflower seeds
¼ cup (20 g) nutritional yeast
3½ tablespoons Miso Mushroom
    Paste (page 57) or red miso
1 tablespoon sesame oil
Finely grated zest and juice of
    2 limes, preferably organic
1 teaspoon soy sauce
1 tablespoon chili-garlic paste
½ dried red chile, crushed

RAMEN
2 tablespoons sesame oil
5 garlic cloves, finely grated
3-inch (8 cm) nub fresh ginger,
    peeled and minced
4 scallions, very thinly sliced
2 tablespoons miso paste
1 tablespoon mirin
4 cups (1 L) mushroom broth, such
    as Everyday Mushroom Broth
    (page 80) or Lion's Mane Broth
    (page 82)
Ramen noodles, for serving

FOR GARNISH
Thinly sliced scallions
Lime wedges
Sesame seeds
Garlic-chili paste
Pickled ginger, radish, and tumeric
Blanched bok choy or spinach

This ramen was developed for my daughter, who loves ramen but lately has preferred to eat vegetarian. I wanted to mimic the thick, rich, glossy broth that comes from the long-cooked meat versions that she loves so much. The mushroom and seaweed dashi add some meatiness and minerality, while the nut butter offers creamy, salty richness, replacing the fat and saltiness that usually comes from an animal protein. When making the seed butter, use a strong food processor—a spice grinder or mini processor may not be powerful enough.

Make the dashi: In a small saucepan, soak the kombu, maitakes, wood ears, and shiitakes in the just-boiled water for 30 minutes.

After 30 minutes, slowly bring the mixture to a bare simmer and simmer for 5 minutes. Remove from the heat and let cool. Discard the kombu. Thinly slice the soaked wood ears and shiitakes and shred the maitakes. Set the mushrooms aside. Reserve the dashi in the saucepan.

Make the ramen base seed butter: In a food processor, combine the nut butter, sunflower seeds, nutritional yeast, miso mushroom paste, oil, lime zest, lime juice, soy sauce, chili-garlic paste, and chile, buzzing until completely smooth. Transfer to a bowl and set aside.

Make the ramen: In a soup pot, heat the oil over medium-low heat. Add the garlic, ginger, and scallions and cook until soft and fragrant, about 5 minutes. Add the miso paste and mirin. Cook, stirring, until the mirin evaporates, 1 to 2 minutes. Stir in the reserved sliced and shredded mushrooms, then the dashi and mushroom broth. Stir in the seed butter. Bring to a bare simmer and cook until hot, about 5 minutes. You want all the ingredients to combine into a smooth soup.

In a separate pot, cook the noodles according to the package directions. Drain.

Divide the noodles among bowls and ladle hot broth into each. Garnish as desired and serve.

5

MUSHROOMS FOR COCKTAIL HOUR

MOTHER MUSHROOM DIPS

I like to serve a big platter of raw vegetables with dips (see photo on page 148) for an evening with friends or during the holiday season, when everyone has had their fill of cheese and cured meat. The mushroom bagna cauda is lovely and garlicky, as are the aioli and the labneh dip. The umami butter and the tapenade are filled with deeply savory, salty flavors. Serve with an assortment of raw vegetables—such as radishes, carrots, cabbage, turnips, kohlrabi, endive, and radicchio.

Brown Butter Porcini Bagna Cauda

MAKES 2 CUPS (285 G)

8 tablespoons (4 oz/115 g) unsalted
    butter, at room temperature
1 cup (240 ml) extra-virgin olive oil
10 garlic cloves, smashed and
    peeled
12 anchovy fillets, chopped
2 tablespoons porcini or maitake
    powder
Assorted crunchy vegetables, for
    dipping

Adding mushroom powder makes this a nontraditional but nonetheless delicious bagna cauda. I serve it as a dip for fresh vegetables but also spoon it over grilled fish, steak, or mushrooms or roasted vegetables, and use it to dress the Salad of Pink Radicchios, Citrus, and Mushroom Bagna Cauda (page 144).

In a medium saucepan, melt the butter over medium-low heat until it starts to brown and smell nutty. The milk solids will start to fall to the bottom of the pan. Watch closely to ensure it doesn't burn. Reduce the heat to the lowest setting and add the oil and garlic. Gently cook until the garlic is soft, 10 to 15 minutes. Add the anchovies and mushroom powder and continue to cook, stirring, until the anchovies melt, about 5 minutes. Mash the softened garlic with a fork to incorporate. Remove the dip from the heat and serve warm, with vegetables.

Umami Mushroom Butter

MAKES ½ CUP (125 G)

1 nori sheet
½ cup (20 g) dried mushrooms
    (cracker-dry) or 1 tablespoon
    mushroom powder
8 tablespoons (4 oz/115 g) unsalted
    butter, at room temperature,
    cut into 1-inch (3 cm) pieces
Flaky sea salt, such as Maldon

I use this flavored butter for raw spring and winter vegetables, but you can use it year-round. I like it on Salty Sour Dark Rye toast (page 73), raw and steamed vegetables, grilled or roasted fish, and as an alternative to the miso mushroom butter for the roast chicken (page 177). It is also delicious melted and tossed with popcorn.

In a dry cast-iron skillet over medium heat, toast the nori sheet for 30 seconds on each side until crispy. Pulse the nori in a food processor or mini chopper. If using dried mushrooms, add them now and pulse everything to a powder. Add the butter (and mushroom powder, if using) and pulse until combined and the mixture is light and fluffy (you may need to scrape down the sides). Add salt to taste. Transfer to a dish and garnish with salt.

Mushroom Aioli

MAKES 1 CUP (ABOUT 200 G)

1 large or 2 small garlic cloves,
   peeled
½ teaspoon Himalayan pink salt
1 tablespoon mushroom powder,
   such as Everyday Mushroom
   Powder (page 50), or shiitake,
   maitake, or porcini powder
1 large organic egg yolk, at room
   temperature
½ cup (120 ml) good-quality extra-
   virgin olive oil
½ cup (120 ml) neutral oil, such as
   grapeseed or avocado
Juice of ½ lemon

Nothing's better than a giant sandwich piled high with juicy August tomatoes, tinged with salt and dripping in homemade aioli. Yes, please! You can, of course, serve this aioli all year long with all kinds of seasonal raw vegetables. Aioli is an essential that is important to master. I make mine by hand because I find it to be meditative, but feel free to use a food processor. Shiitake or porcini powder is nice here, but you can experiment with other cultivated or wild dried mushroom powders. Fat (in this case, from the olive oil and egg yolk) loves to take on flavor, so any type of earthy, flavorful mushroom will shine.

By hand: Place the garlic and salt in a large mortar (large enough to hold at least 2 cups/480 ml). With the pestle, grind the salt and garlic to a paste. Add the mushroom powder and incorporate into the garlic paste. Add the egg yolk, whisking to combine everything together. Combine both oils in a liquid measuring cup or any cup with a spout. Now begin to add the oil VERY slowly (literally drop by drop; this will ensure the emulsion doesn't separate). Continue to add the oil slowly, whisking vigorously until the yolk and oil emulsify and start to thicken. When the mixture has reached the desired thickness, add the lemon juice, whisking to combine.

By machine: Finely grate the garlic with a Microplane zester. Place the egg yolk in a food processor and buzz for 25 to 30 seconds. Add the garlic, salt, lemon juice, and mushroom powder and buzz for another 25 to 30 seconds. Combine both oils in a liquid measuring cup or any cup with a spout. With the machine running, slowly drizzle in the oil, drop by drop at first, and then in a very thin, steady stream. The stream should be somewhere between the diameter of a needle and a small porcupine quill. The process should take anywhere from 3 to 7 minutes from start to finish, depending on your machine.

Serve the aioli immediately or cover and store in the refrigerator until ready to serve. It should keep for up to 4 days in the refrigerator.

Mushroom Olive Caper Tapenade

MAKES 2½ CUPS (455 G)

½ pound (225 g) mixed mushrooms,
    trimmed and cut into small
    pieces

½ cup (75 g) pitted Kalamata olives,
    sliced or torn in half

½ cup (75 g) pitted Castelvetrano
    olives

2 tablespoons capers in brine,
    rinsed

4 garlic cloves, smashed and
    peeled

1 small shallot, thinly sliced

½ teaspoon Aleppo pepper or
    ½ dried red chile, such as chile
    de árbol, crushed, plus more
    for garnish

¼ teaspoon Himalayan pink salt

¼ teaspoon coarsely ground black
    pepper, plus more for garnish

6 tablespoons extra-virgin olive oil,
    plus more for storing

¼ cup (25 g) walnut halves

¼ teaspoon cumin seeds

½ cup (20 g) coarsely chopped
    fresh flat-leaf parsley leaves

Finely grated zest and juice of
    1 lemon, preferably organic

Crackers, crostini, and crunchy
    vegetables, for serving

This dip is full of deep, layered, umami flavor due to the roasting of the mushrooms, olives, capers, and shallot. It's as delicious smeared on bread or crackers as it is with vegetables for dipping. The flavors mellow a bit if made a day or two ahead of serving.

Preheat the oven to 400°F (200°C). Line a baking sheet with parchment paper.

In a large bowl, combine the mushrooms, both olives, the capers, garlic, shallot, Aleppo pepper, salt, black pepper, and 2 tablespoons of the oil. Mix with your hands to evenly coat. Arrange in an even layer on the lined baking sheet. Roast until the mushrooms have softened and are beginning to get crisp, about 15 minutes. Set aside to cool on the baking sheet.

In a small dry cast-iron skillet over medium heat, toast the walnut halves and cumin seeds until fragrant, about 1 minute, taking care not to let them burn. Set aside to cool.

On a cutting board, combine the toasted walnut mixture with the mushroom mixture and coarsely chop them together. (I prefer a rustic chop, so I do it by hand. If you use a food processor, pulse rather than process, so you don't puree it.)

Transfer to a serving bowl and add the parsley, lemon zest, lemon juice, and 2 tablespoons oil, stirring to combine. Garnish with a pinch of Aleppo pepper and a little cracked black pepper and drizzle with the remaining 2 tablespoons oil.

Serve immediately with crackers, crostini, and vegetables. To store, place in a glass jar and cover with a thin layer of oil. The tapenade should keep in the refrigerator for up to 2 weeks.

Mushroom Labneh Dip

MAKES 1½ CUPS (385 G)

1 cup (240 g) labneh
3 tablespoons buttermilk
2 tablespoons extra-virgin olive oil,
    plus more for drizzling
¼ preserved lemon, store-bought
    or homemade (page 94), seeded
    and finely chopped
Finely grated zest and juice of
    1 lemon, preferably organic
1½ tablespoons mushroom
    powder, any variety, store-
    bought or homemade (page 50)
¼ teaspoon chile flakes or ¼ dried
    chile de árbol
¼ teaspoon Himalayan pink salt

This dip doubles as a nice sauce for Shiitake Kofta (page 140), Mixed Mushroom Pakora (page 154), or the Salt and Pepper Brick Mushrooms (page 202).

In a small bowl, whisk together all the ingredients until smooth. Drizzle with oil and serve.

MIXED MUSHROOM PAKORA

SERVES 6 TO 8

¼ teaspoon cumin seeds
¼ teaspoon black mustard seeds
1 cup (90 g) chickpea flour
¼ teaspoon ground coriander
¼ teaspoon ground Kashmiri chile
¼ teaspoon ground turmeric
½ teaspoon Himalayan pink salt
1 tablespoon nutritional yeast
Finely grated zest and juice of
    1 lemon, preferably organic
1 garlic clove, finely grated with
    a Microplane
1 tablespoon grated fresh ginger
1½ cups (360 ml) buttermilk, plus
    more if needed
1½ pounds (680 g) mixed
    mushrooms, such as enoki,
    white or brown beech (Bunapi),
    maitake, and lion's mane
Neutral oil, such as safflower, for
    deep-frying
Flaky sea salt, such as Maldon,
    or Mushroom Salt (page 53), for
    sprinkling
Crushed red chile, for serving
Cilantro Mint Chutney (page 89),
    for serving
Lime or lemon wedges, for serving

Every culture has a type of fritter, and pakora is one of my favorites. It hails from India, where the popular street food is often eaten with a steaming, barely-able-to-hold glass of masala chai. In India, many different vegetables are fried for pakora, but I like to use a variety of mushrooms. The mushrooms are bathed in a chickpea batter loaded with spices and zesty ginger. With the addition of citrus and buttermilk, the batter becomes a little tangy. The mushrooms are fried to golden crispness and served with a flavorful homemade chutney.

In a small dry cast-iron skillet over medium-low heat, toast the cumin and black mustard seeds until fragrant and the mustard seeds begin to pop, about 1 minute.

In a large bowl, stir together the chickpea flour, coriander, chile, turmeric, pink salt, and nutritional yeast. Add the lemon zest, lemon juice, garlic, and ginger, stirring to combine. Stir in the toasted cumin and mustard seeds. Add the buttermilk little by little, just enough to be as thick as a pancake batter (if the batter is still too thick, add more buttermilk, but the batter should not be runny). Set the batter aside.

Clean and trim any hard mushroom stems, then slice, cut, or tear into pieces 2½ to 3 inches (6 to 8 cm) long. If using lion's mane or maitake, gently tear into medium pieces.

Line one large or two small baking sheets with parchment paper. Working in batches, dip the mushrooms in the batter, letting excess drip back into the bowl, and set aside on the baking sheet(s).

Line a large plate with a paper towel or clean brown paper bag. In a deep, heavy-bottomed pot, heat 2 inches (5 cm) oil until the temperature reaches 350°F (177°C). Working with 2 or 3 pieces at a time (to avoid crowding the pot), fry the mushrooms until golden and crispy, about 2 minutes. Remove with a slotted spoon and transfer to the lined plate to drain. Sprinkle with flaky salt and crushed chile.

Serve the pakora warm, with the chutney and lime wedges.

KING TRUMPET CHIPS WITH CREAMY LEEK AND GARLIC CHIVE DIP

SERVES 4

1 cup (240 g) labneh

¼ cup (5 g) dried leeks (see page 41), plus more for garnish (optional)

1 tablespoon dried garlic chives (see page 41)

1 tablespoon nutritional yeast

½ teaspoon ramp salt or any other allium salt

1 to 2 tablespoons whole-milk yogurt

2 cups (480 ml) grapeseed or other neutral oil, for frying

½ pound (225 g) king trumpet (king oyster) mushrooms, trimmed and very thinly sliced lengthwise on the thinnest setting on a mandoline

Flaky sea salt, such as Maldon, for sprinkling

Very thinly sliced king trumpet mushrooms (also known as king oyster) turn beautifully crispy and super tasty when fried in neutral oil. I like to serve them with a creamy leek-and-garlic labneh that's a healthier riff on my all-time favorite dip, sour cream and onion. The first step is to dehydrate leeks and garlic chives, which seems like a challenge but is quite easy; see How to Dry Leeks (page 41) for the method.

In a small bowl, combine the labneh, dried leeks, dried garlic chives, nutritional yeast, and ramp salt. Stir in the yogurt to thin the dip, as needed.

Line a sheet pan with paper towels and set near the stove (the mushrooms cook really quickly, so you have to be ready). In a deep, heavy-bottomed pot, heat 3 inches (8 cm) oil until the temperature reaches 350°F (177°C). If you don't have a thermometer, you can test by dropping a piece of mushroom into the oil; if it sizzles, it's ready.

Working in batches to avoid crowding the pot, drop the mushroom slices into the hot oil and fry until they turn golden, about 1 minute. With a slotted spoon, transfer the chips to the paper towels to drain.

Sprinkle the chips with flaky salt and dried leeks (if desired) and serve with the dip.

HERBY MUSHROOM DUMPLINGS

MAKES ABOUT 60 DUMPLINGS

DUMPLINGS

2 tablespoons sesame oil

1 large shallot, minced (about ½ cup/70 g)

1 pound (455 g) mixed fresh shiitake and maitake mushrooms, trimmed and coarsely chopped (not too big, but not minced)

2-inch (5 cm) nub fresh ginger, peeled and finely grated with a Microplane

2 garlic cloves, finely grated with a Microplane

½ cup (20 g) coarsely chopped garlic greens, spring onion, garlic chives, or chives

3 tablespoons dark soy sauce

2 tablespoons fish sauce, such as Red Boat

½ tablespoon Miso Mushroom Paste (page 57)

1 tablespoon maple syrup

¼ teaspoon chili-garlic sauce

4 cups (4 oz/115 g) finely chopped spinach, nettles, chrysanthemum, chard, or dandelion greens

½ cup (15 g) fresh mint leaves, coarsely chopped

½ cup (15 g) fresh cilantro, coarsely chopped

Finely grated zest and juice of ½ lemon, preferably organic

Two 10-ounce (284 g) packages round dumpling wrappers

Black sesame seeds, for dipping

FOR FRYING AND SERVING

Neutral oil, such as safflower

Finely chopped garlic greens (or garlic chives), cilantro, spring onion, chives, or scallions

Yuzu Chili-Garlic Soy Dipping Sauce (page 89)

When my kids were little, we often made pork-and-chive dumplings on New Year's Day. Now we generally pan-fry these mushroom dumplings (although you can steam them). The filling has a meaty texture—so much so that the most avid carnivores won't even realize it's just deliciously mutable fungi. The dipping sauce is key: Yuzu juice keeps it bright and citrusy, and chili-garlic sauce gives it a definite zing! This recipe makes a lot of dumplings, but they freeze quite well, which comes in handy when you want to satisfy any midnight dumpling cravings.

Make the dumplings: In a large Dutch oven or cast-iron skillet, heat the sesame oil over medium heat until it starts to shimmer. Add the shallot and cook until soft, translucent, and starting to brown at the edges, 3 to 5 minutes. Stir in the mushrooms, ginger, garlic, garlic greens, soy sauce, fish sauce, miso mushroom paste, maple syrup, and chili-garlic sauce. Cook until soft, stirring occasionally, 5 to 7 minutes.

Add the spinach and cook just until wilted, a minute or two. Remove from the heat and let cool. Add the mint and cilantro, and finish with the lemon zest and lemon juice, tossing to combine.

Working with one wrapper at a time, place a heaping tablespoon of filling in the center. Fold two sides together and carefully pleat and pinch the dough to enclose the filling. Lightly brush the bottom with a little water and dip into a bowl of black sesame seeds. Transfer the dumplings directly onto a sheet pan. Repeat with the remaining wrappers and filling, keeping them in a single layer. If not cooking right away, freeze the dumplings on the sheet pan. Once frozen, transfer them to a zip-top bag and store in the freezer for up to 6 months.

Fry and serve the dumplings: In a large cast-iron or nonstick skillet, heat 1 tablespoon neutral oil over medium-low heat until shimmering. Working in batches, arrange the dumplings in an even layer in the pan and cook until just starting to brown on the bottom. Add ¼ cup (60 ml) water—stand back as you pour the water in and keep a lid in your other hand. The water will splatter, so quickly cover the pan with the lid. Steam the dumplings for 4 minutes, or until all the water has evaporated. Repeat using 1 tablespoon oil and ¼ cup (60 ml) water for each batch.

Garnish the dumplings with chopped garlic greens. Serve with the dipping sauce.

MUSHROOMS FOR COCKTAIL HOUR

BROWN BUTTER MUSHROOM CAKES

MAKES 6 CAKES

½ pound (225 g) fresh lion's
  mane mushrooms
2 tablespoons unsalted butter
1½ teaspoons Miso Mushroom
  Paste (page 57)
1 large egg
1¼ cups (140 g) panko bread
  crumbs
½ cup (20 g) coarsely chopped
  fresh flat-leaf parsley
Grated zest and juice of 1 lemon,
  preferably organic
1 garlic clove, finely grated with
  a Microplane
¼ teaspoon chili-garlic sauce
2 tablespoons mayonnaise
1 teaspoon mustard powder
¼ teaspoon celery seed
¼ teaspoon Himalayan pink salt
¼ teaspoon coarsely ground
  black pepper
½ teaspoon flaky sea salt, such
  as Maldon
½ cup (120 ml) neutral oil, for
  frying
Lemon wedges, for serving
Briny Yogurt Tartar Sauce (page
  86), for serving

These cocktail-hour appetizers hit all the notes of a crab cake, right down to the texture of the lion's mane mushrooms, which shred like crab and are said to have a mild seafood flavor. While I like the idea of eating crab cakes, I am honestly more into the tartar sauce and lemon wedges that accompany them. (I am a condiment person.) Make the sauce before you start to assemble the cakes.

Gently shred the mushrooms to resemble crabmeat, then coarsely chop to give the mixture a slightly irregular texture and shorten some of the longer pieces.

In a small cast-iron skillet, combine the butter and miso mushroom paste and heat over medium-low heat, stirring. The butter will foam up as it begins to brown, and the butter solids will fall to the bottom of the pan. Continue to stir until the butter is browned, about 4 minutes. Add the mushrooms and cook until soft and golden brown all over, 2 to 3 minutes. Remove from the heat and let cool.

In a large bowl, stir together the egg, ½ cup (55 g) of the panko, the parsley, lemon zest, lemon juice, garlic, chili-garlic sauce, mayonnaise, mustard powder, celery seed, pink salt, and pepper. Add the cooled mushrooms, tossing to combine.

Line a small sheet pan with parchment paper. Using your hands, divide the mushroom mixture into 6 portions and form into patties about 2½ inches (6 cm) across and ½ inch (1 cm) thick.

In a large shallow bowl, combine the remaining ¾ cup (85 g) panko and the flaky salt. Working with one at a time, gently pick up a patty and dip it into the panko mixture, making sure to coat it completely on both sides. Transfer to the parchment-lined sheet as you work. Refrigerate the patties on the baking sheet until well chilled, 30 minutes to 1 hour.

Line a large plate with a paper towel. In a medium skillet, heat the oil over medium until shimmering but not smoking.

Working in batches, fry the patties until the undersides are browned and crisp, about 5 minutes. Flip and brown the other side, about 5 minutes longer. Transfer to the paper towel to drain slightly.

Serve the cakes warm with lemon wedges and tartar sauce.

TOAST WITH ROASTED GRAPES, SOFT CHEESE, AND TRUFFLE

SERVES 4

½ pound (225 g) seedless grapes, stems on

A few fresh oregano sprigs

1 tablespoon extra-virgin olive oil, plus more for serving

¼ teaspoon fennel pollen

4 slices Salty Sour Dark Rye (page 73) or crusty sourdough bread

¼ pound (115 g) soft cheese, such as blue cheese (Bayley Hazen or Jasper Hill), triple crème such as brie, or goat cheese

1 black truffle

Adaptogenic Mushroom Honey (page 58), for serving

Flaky sea salt, such as Maldon, for serving

Truffles are super special and should be treated as such. I like to serve them with roasted fruit—in this case, seedless grapes roasted at a high temperature with a trace of fragrant floral fennel pollen and a little olive oil. I arrange the grapes over toasted bread smeared with creamy soft cheese and top it all off with some shavings of truffle and a drizzle of adaptogenic honey. If you can't get your hands on a truffle, use any wild mushrooms, sautéed in butter, in its place. Serve with a nice funky orange wine or a glass of Cava and some cracked walnuts.

Preheat the oven to 425°F (220°C).

Place the grapes on a large baking sheet. Arrange the oregano sprigs among the grapes. Drizzle with the oil and sprinkle with the fennel pollen. Roast until the grapes are soft and start to split, about 20 minutes.

Meanwhile, toast the bread and slather with a smear of soft cheese.

Top the toasts with the roasted grapes (or serve alongside). Shave 2 or 3 pieces of truffle on top. Finish with drizzles of oil and honey, and a sprinkle of salt.

COOKING WITH MUSHROOMS

SPIRITS INFUSED WITH SHIITAKE AND MAITAKE

MAKES ABOUT 3 CUPS (720 ML)

3 cups (720 ml) gin or mezcal
1 cup (1¼ oz/35 g) dried whole
  shiitake mushrooms
⅓ cup (about ½ oz/18 g) dried
  maitake mushroom pieces

I love experimenting with infused spirits, but infusing with mushrooms is something I had never done until recently. I wasn't sure if the mushroom would come forward in the way that infused citrus, herbs, or fruits do, but I was pleasantly surprised by the earthiness that emerged. Vodka is the best choice for infused spirits, as it's the "cleanest," meaning it's essentially flavorless. However, I am much more of a mezcal or gin drinker when I reach for a cocktail, so that's what I used here. The herbaceous, botanical profile of gin paired well with mushrooms, while the smoky mezcal added a more layered and grounded taste.

Pour the gin or mezcal into a 2-quart (2 L) glass canning jar with a tight-fitting lid. Add the dried mushrooms and stir to mix.

Let the gin infuse in a cool, dark place at room temperature for at least 1 month and up to 3 months. The spirits will take on an amber color from the mushrooms.

Pour the alcohol and mushrooms through a fine-mesh sieve set over a cleaned 1-quart (1 L) glass jar. With clean hands, squeeze as much liquid out of the mushrooms as possible. (The spongy mushrooms will have absorbed much of the alcohol.) Store at room temperature, away from heat and light.

THREE COCKTAILS

I have started to see commercially produced mushroom-infused spirits in the market (see the Source Guide, page 232), so if you'd prefer, you can purchase them rather than make your own to use in the cocktail recipes that follow.

Mushroom Negroni

MAKES 1 COCKTAIL

1 ounce (30 ml) mushroom-infused
    gin (see page 165)
1 ounce (30 ml) sweet vermouth
1 ounce (30 ml) Campari
Wide strip of orange peel, for garnish

Pour the gin, vermouth, and Campari into a cocktail glass with ice. Stir to combine and garnish with the orange peel.

Mezcal Mushroom Margarita

MAKES 1 COCKTAIL

2 ounces (60 ml) fresh lime juice,
    plus more for rimming the glass
Mushroom Salt (page 153), for
    rimming the glass
½ ounce (15 ml) agave syrup or
    maple syrup
1 ounce (30 ml) Cointreau
2 ounces (60 ml) mushroom-
    infused mezcal (see page 165)

Dip the rim of a highball or other cocktail glass in some lime juice and a plate of mushroom salt and set aside.

In a cocktail shaker filled with ice, combine the lime juice, agave, Cointreau, and mezcal and shake or stir. Strain into the rimmed glass and serve straight up or on the rocks.

Mushroom French 75

MAKES 1 COCKTAIL

2 ounces (60 ml) mushroom-
    infused gin (see page 165)
1 ounce (30 ml) fresh lemon juice
1 ounce (30 ml) agave syrup
2 ounces (60 ml) Prosecco or
    sparkling orange wine
Wide strip of lemon peel, for garnish

In a cocktail shaker filled with ice, combine the gin, lemon juice, and agave. Shake well until very cold, 25 to 30 seconds. Strain into a coupe glass, top off with Prosecco, and garnish with the lemon peel.

MUSHROOMS FOR COCKTAIL HOUR

6

DINNER FROM MUSHROOMS

ENOKI ALFREDO

SERVES 2

Coarse salt
1 pound (455 g) enoki mushrooms
4 tablespoons (2 oz/60 g) unsalted
    butter, cut into 1-tablespoon
    pieces
2 ounces (60 g) finely grated
    parmesan (you should get a
    little more than ½ cup)
1 teaspoon cracked black pepper
Freshly grated nutmeg
Extra-virgin olive oil, for drizzling

Enoki mushrooms grow in a bundle of ghostly white strands. Once trimmed, each bundle can be separated into a pile of individual mushrooms. They are delicate and a little crunchy when cooked. When thrown into salted boiling water, the mushrooms take on an angel hair pasta–like appearance. This dish is an incredibly simple nod to two classic Italian pastas, Alfredo and cacio e pepe, with just a handful of ingredients: enoki, butter, parmesan, black pepper, grated nutmeg, and a drizzle of olive oil at the finish, for extra gloss. It's a perfect recipe for anyone who doesn't eat gluten but wants the indulgence of saucy, creamy pasta for dinner. Could enoki be the new spaghetti squash? Perhaps!

Bring a pot of generously salted water to a boil.

Trim the enoki and separate the strands into piles. Cook the mushrooms in the boiling water for 1½ minutes. Reserve ¼ cup (60 ml) cooking liquid and drain the mushrooms.

Return the mushrooms to the pot. Add the butter, stirring until melted. Add the parmesan and stir vigorously until the sauce is glossy and creamy. Add a little of the reserved cooking water, if needed.

Top with pepper, a scant grating of nutmeg, and a drizzle of oil, and serve.

COOKING WITH MUSHROOMS

BIGOLI IN SALSA WITH MAITAKE

SERVES 4 TO 6

3 tablespoons unsalted butter

2 tablespoons extra-virgin olive oil, plus more for drizzling

1 pound (455 g) yellow onions, very thinly sliced into half-moons (use a mandoline if you have one)

½ cup (120 ml) water

½ pound (225 g) fresh maitake, chanterelle, or chestnut mushrooms, trimmed and gently torn or thinly sliced

13 oil-packed anchovy fillets or sardines

4 tablespoons dry white wine

Coarse salt

½ pound (225 g) thick spaghetti (farro, buckwheat, or whole wheat) or bigoli (if you are lucky enough to find it!)

1 teaspoon ume plum vinegar

¼ cup (15 g) finely chopped fresh flat-leaf parsley

Coarsely ground black pepper

Flaky sea salt, such as Maldon

Everyone has that one pasta dish to satisfy all the cravings, and bigoli in salsa is mine. The recipe takes some time to make, as the onions cook down very slowly, until they almost melt. I first tasted it late one night in Venice, and ate it every night thereafter until I left a week later. Bigoli in salsa was popularized by Venetian fishermen and was typically made with salted anchovies and sometimes sardines, either salt-cured or oil-packed. The beauty of this dish is that it has only a few ingredients: onions, tinned fish, white wine, black pepper, and bigoli, a thick-strand pasta traditionally made with buckwheat flour and duck eggs. If you can't find it, substitute fat spaghetti or bucatini made with farro or whole wheat; either will give it the signature nuttiness that balances the sweetness of the long-cooked onions. I add ume plum vinegar for a touch of acid, but you can add a splash of apple cider vinegar in its place.

The biggest adaptation I have made to bigoli in salsa, however, is adding mushrooms. They bring an earthiness to the sweet-savory-umami combination of flavors. You can use a variety of mushrooms; I like maitakes, but chanterelles and chestnut mushrooms also work well. The pasta water, onions, and fish melt together into a rich sauce that will transport you right to the canals of Venice.

In an 8- to 12-inch (20 to 30 cm) skillet or sauté pan, heat 1 tablespoon of the butter and the oil over medium-low heat until the butter melts. Add the onions and cook until soft, 15 to 20 minutes.

Add the water, cover, and cook, stirring occasionally, until the onions are beginning to melt and fall apart, 25 to 30 minutes longer.

Stir in the mushrooms, anchovy fillets, and 2 tablespoons of the wine. Cook until the anchovies have disintegrated and the mushrooms are super soft, another 15 minutes. Remove from the heat and set aside.

Meanwhile, bring a large pot of salted water to a boil. Add the pasta and cook until al dente according to the package directions. Reserve 1 cup (240 ml) pasta water and drain the pasta.

Just before draining the pasta, heat the mushroom mixture over low heat. Add 1 tablespoon of the butter, the vinegar, and the remaining 2 tablespoons wine. Stir to combine. Once the butter has melted and the wine has reduced, remove from the heat.

Add the drained pasta to the onion-mushroom mixture in the sauté pan along with the remaining 1 tablespoon butter. Cook over medium heat, adding some of the reserved pasta water a little at a time, until the sauce is glossy, 1 to 2 minutes. Toss with the parsley and serve immediately, garnished with pepper, a little flaky salt, and a drizzle of oil.

LEEK-MUSHROOM RISOTTO

SERVES 4

6 cups (1.4 L) mushroom broth ,
    such as Everyday Mushroom
    Broth (page 80) or Lion's Mane
    Broth (page 82)
½ ounce (15 g) dried porcinis
¼ cup (60 ml) extra-virgin olive oil,
    plus more for drizzling
6 tablespoons (3 oz/85 g) unsalted
    butter
1 large or 2 small leeks, thinly
    sliced and well washed (about
    2 cups/180 g)
1 small shallot, minced
1¼ cups (240 g) short-grain rice,
    such as Arborio
1 cup (240 ml) dry white wine
1 bunch fresh flat-leaf parsley,
    coarsely chopped (about
    ½ cup/25 g)
¼ pound (115 g) fresh maitake
    mushrooms, shredded into
    medium-small pieces
½ tablespoon mushroom powder,
    any variety
1 cup (20 g) dried leeks
    (see page 41)
1½ teaspoons finely chopped
    preserved lemon, preferably
    Meyer lemon, store-bought or
    homemade (page 94)
1 cup (100 g) finely grated pecorino
    or parmesan cheese, plus more
    for serving
Himalayan pink salt
Coarsely ground black pepper
1 lemon, halved

Risotto is one of the first dishes I made after studying for a semester in Italy. Before then, I had the misconstrued idea that the dish required intense concentration and staying put at the stove, stirring, stirring, stirring. It is true that you must stir risotto, and it is a commitment, but it's not a laborious one. Now I will happily stand at the stove as the smell of the mushrooms, shallots, and leeks begins to bloom and the motions of stirring and adding stock become a beautiful dance. I used dried and fresh mushrooms here as well as preserved lemon to add a bright, citrusy note. Serve the risotto when it is still a little soupy (it will set up as it cools). The rice should be soft with a toothsome chew (al dente). It is done when you can drag the spoon across the bottom of the pan and the trail of the spoon remains visible.

In a pot, heat the broth and keep it at a bare simmer and ready for ladling into the rice.

Remove 1 cup (240 ml) hot broth and soak the dried porcinis in it for 15 to 20 minutes. Remove the porcinis with a slotted spoon and set aside. Strain the broth through a fine-mesh sieve to remove any grit and return it to the pot. Coarsely chop the soaked porcinis.

In a large saucepan, heat the oil and 3 tablespoons of the butter over medium heat until the butter is melted. Add the fresh leek and shallot and cook until translucent and soft but not browned, about 5 minutes.

Add the rice and cook, stirring, until coated and toasted, about 5 minutes.

Add the wine and 1 tablespoon of the butter and stir until all the liquid is absorbed, scraping the pan to incorporate all the toasty bits and butter solids. Stir in the parsley, maitakes, chopped porcinis, mushroom powder, dried leeks, and preserved lemon.

Add the hot stock, about ½ cup (120 ml) at a time; you will want to stir so all of the liquid gets nearly absorbed before adding the next ladleful. Repeat until the rice is al dente, 30 to 40 minutes.

Remove from the heat. Add the cheese and remaining 2 tablespoons butter, stirring to incorporate. The risotto should be plenty salty from the pecorino and preserved lemon, but adjust the salt as needed.

Transfer the risotto to a large shallow platter and hit with a drizzle of oil, some pepper, and a squeeze of lemon.

COOKING WITH MUSHROOMS

ROAST CHICKEN WITH MISO MUSHROOM BUTTER

SERVES 4 GENEROUSLY

Kosher salt

1 whole chicken (3½ to 4 lb/1.6 to 1.8 kg), preferably organic, patted dry

Miso Mushroom Butter (page 57), at room temperature

1 lemon, preferably organic, halved

15 Yukon Gold potatoes (about 3 lb/1.4 kg total)

2 pounds (910 g) fresh mushrooms, such as oyster, maitake, or chanterelle, cleaned and trimmed

Coarsely ground black pepper

Extra-virgin olive oil, for drizzling

Note: To "turn" a potato, as you remove the skin with a paring knife, shape it so it's thicker in the center and tapered at the end (imagine a barrel shape with 6 to 8 sides).

There are probably a thousand ways or more to roast a chicken. Ask anyone and they will tell you a different story. In my family, we like a well-done bird with crispy skin. It took me a long time to get to a recipe I am happy with. Pre-salting the chicken and letting it rest overnight in the fridge is something I learned from the late Judy Rodgers of Zuni Café in San Francisco, when we photographed her cookbook. Here the copious amount of miso mushroom butter is key to giving this bird its juicy, buttery, crispy texture. The butter is placed under the loosened skin of the breast and thighs. I truss the bird to keep it neatly tucked; otherwise, the butter escapes too quickly. The initial high heat followed by the lower temperature perfectly cooks the chicken. As the miso mushroom butter flavors the chicken, it slowly drips down onto the mushrooms and potatoes, creating a perfect roast, creamy browned potatoes, and crispy, buttery, schmaltzy mushrooms. (Truth be told, this is my go-to roast chicken recipe even without the potatoes and mushrooms.) Flipping it over and then back again gets the bottom nicely browned.

Salt the chicken liberally inside and out, using about 1 teaspoon salt per pound (455 g). Place the chicken on a small baking sheet and refrigerate uncovered overnight.

Remove the chicken from the fridge. Gently slide your hands between the skin of the breast all the way to the back and down the sides. With your fingers, loosen the skin from the inside around the legs.

Taking care not to tear the skin, pack the miso mushroom butter under the skin, all the way to the legs, making sure to cover the top and bottom legs and wings. Stuff the cavity with the lemon halves and then truss the bird. Set the bird aside to come to room temperature, about 1½ hours.

Position a rack in the center of the oven and preheat the oven to 475°F (245°C).

Bring a large pot of water to a boil and season well with salt. Peel the potatoes in the French tourné style (aka "turned" potatoes; see Note). Parboil the potatoes until just soft enough to pierce with a fork, 10 to 12 minutes.

Meanwhile, chop or shred the mushrooms and place on a large sheet pan.

Drain the potatoes and transfer to the center of the pan with the mushrooms. Set the chicken on top of the mushrooms and potatoes.

(continued)

Top with a few turns of pepper and a drizzle of oil, making sure to get the chicken, potatoes, and mushrooms.

Transfer to the oven and roast for 20 minutes.

Reduce the oven temperature to 350°F (177°C). Flip the bird over and roast for 20 minutes to brown the bottom. At that point, turn it right side up again and roast for another 40 to 50 minutes, depending on the size of the bird. (The total cooking time, including the 20 minutes at high heat, will be 80 to 90 minutes.) When the chicken is done, the joints and legs will be loose and the juices will run clear.

Remove the pan from the oven. Transfer the chicken to a wire rack set on another sheet pan. Return the pan with the mushrooms and potatoes to the oven. Increase the heat to 400°F (200°C) and turn the potatoes and mushrooms so they get coated in the juices. Roast until browned, 15 to 20 minutes.

Transfer the potatoes and mushrooms to a large serving platter. Remove the lemon from the chicken cavity, scoop out the flesh of the lemon, and toss with the mushrooms and potatoes.

At this point, the chicken should be cool enough to carve (and the juices will be set). Carve the chicken, transferring pieces to the platter with the potatoes and mushrooms. Pour the pan juices over everything, and serve immediately.

SWEET AND SOUR MUSHROOM PUMPKIN CURRY

SERVES 6

6 tablespoons boiling water

3 tablespoons tamarind pulp (see Note, next page), from a pliable block

1 small or ½ medium kabocha squash (2 to 2½ lb/910 g to 1.1 kg)

½ pound (225 g) fresh mushrooms, such as chestnut, white or brown beech (Bunapi), or maitake

¼ cup plus 2 tablespoons water

1 tablespoon jaggery powder

½ cup (45 g) grated fresh coconut or frozen grated coconut

1 teaspoon ground coriander

¾ teaspoon Himalayan pink salt, plus more to taste

4 garlic cloves, finely chopped (about 2 tablespoons)

2½-inch (6 cm) nub fresh ginger, peeled and minced (about 2 tablespoons)

¼ cup (60 ml) organic coconut oil

1 teaspoon black mustard seeds

¼ teaspoon fenugreek seeds

1 large or 2 small shallots, thinly sliced

14 fresh curry leaves, rinsed

1 fresh green chile, seeded and minced

2 tablespoons ground turmeric

4 cups (1 L) mushroom broth, such as Everyday Mushroom Broth (page 80) or Lion's Mane Broth (page 82)

One 13-ounce (385 ml) can coconut milk

½ cup (60 g) cashews, toasted

Grated zest and juice of 1 lime, preferably organic

This beautiful, brothy stew is inspired by a cooking class I took on Kayal Island in Kerala, India, home to some incredible fisherwomen. There we made a fish curry, typical for South India, but I have since adapted the ingredients to be vegetarian and adjusted the flavor to be a bit more sweet and sour. Before I traveled to Kayal, I was always too intimidated to make a curry. What I discovered is that curries are surprisingly easy to make. I recommend laying out all your measured ingredients in small bowls before you start, as everything comes together rather quickly. What I love about this one is that it is so easy to adapt to any protein or vegetable. The sweetness of the kabocha pairs beautifully with any earthy mushroom. The tamarind and lemon add a little acid, balancing the sweetness of the coconut. The stew makes ahead nicely and freezes well.

In a medium bowl, combine the boiling water with the tamarind pulp, mashing to fully incorporate the two. Let sit for 15 minutes, then strain through a fine-mesh sieve set over a bowl, pushing on the solids. Discard any strings, seeds, or pieces of pod and set aside the tamarind puree.

Cut the squash into wedges, leaving the skin on, then cut into bite-size cubes (about 4 cups/460 g). If using chestnut mushrooms, clean and trim the ends of the mushroom to remove any dirt or substrate. If using beech mushrooms, trim and separate into strands. If using maitakes, gently shred. Set the mushrooms aside.

In a food processor, combine the water, jaggery, grated coconut, coriander, and ¼ teaspoon of the salt and pulse together. Scrape out the coconut paste and set aside.

Add the garlic and ginger to the food processor and pulse just to blend together. (Or pound in a mortar and pestle.)

In a clay pot, donabe, or heavy-bottomed pot, heat the oil over medium heat until it shimmers. Add the mustard seeds and fenugreek seeds and heat until they pop or dance a little in the pan. Add the ginger-garlic mixture, the shallots, curry leaves, and chile. Cook until the shallots are translucent, 4 to 5 minutes. Stir in the turmeric. Add 1 cup (240 ml) of the mushroom broth and cook for 2 to 3 minutes.

Add the reserved coconut paste, the remaining 3 cups (760 ml) broth, the fresh mushrooms, kabocha, 3 tablespoons tamarind puree, and the remaining ½ teaspoon salt. Reduce the heat to low and let the curry gently simmer undisturbed until the squash is fork-tender, about 25 minutes.

(continued)

COOKING WITH MUSHROOMS

FOR SERVING
3 tablespoons ghee
6 fresh curry leaves, rinsed
½ teaspoon black mustard seeds
Cooked brown or black rice
2 limes, cut into wedges
Coriander Yogurt (page 85)
Fresh cilantro

Add the coconut milk and cashews. Return to a simmer and cook for 10 minutes, gently stirring to combine. (You don't want to stir it too much, to keep the mushrooms and squash from becoming mushy.)

Remove from the heat. Add the lime zest and lime juice, cover, and set aside while you make the garnish and rice.

To serve: In a small skillet, heat the ghee over medium-low heat. Add the curry leaves and cook until crisp and dark green, about 1 minute. Remove with a slotted spoon and set aside. Add the mustard seeds and cook until they pop, about 1 minute.

Serve the curry over the rice, with the curry leaf mixture, a big squeeze of lime, a little coriander yogurt, and some fresh cilantro.

Note: I use tamarind pulp in this recipe, which is a pressed cake of tamarind fruit pulp, including the strings and seeds. To use it, you mix it with boiling water and then strain out the seeds, strings, and any pieces of pod to make a puree to add to the curry. I do not recommend using tamarind paste or concentrate in its place.

MUSHROOM PARM

SERVES 6

MUSHROOMS

1½ pounds (680 g) fresh maitake
    mushrooms
¼ cup (60 ml) extra-virgin olive oil
½ teaspoon Himalayan pink salt
A couple turns of black pepper
2 cups (225 g) panko bread crumbs

SAUCE

One 28-ounce (795 g) can whole
    plum tomatoes (I like Italian
    brands; they are more tender
    and soft)
One 14-ounce (411 g) can whole
    plum tomatoes (preferably an
    Italian brand)
¼ cup (60 ml) extra-virgin olive oil
8 garlic cloves, smashed and
    peeled
2 tablespoons fresh oregano
    leaves (or 1 tablespoon dried,
    preferably Sicilian)
20 Castelvetrano green olives,
    pitted and coarsely chopped
1 tablespoon capers (I use the ones
    in olive oil; if using capers in
    brine or salt, rinse and dry)
½ teaspoon Himalayan pink salt,
    plus more to taste

FOR ASSEMBLY

1 pound (455 g) fresh whole-milk
    mozzarella, cut into thin slices
1 cup (100 g) finely grated
    parmesan cheese
1 tablespoon fresh oregano
    leaves (or 1½ teaspoons dried,
    preferably Sicilian)

This no-fry maitake parm makes a nice alternative to the eggplant version, which I sometimes find cumbersome to prepare. The breading and frying and all that olive oil make it rich and tasty but quite heavy. The panko coating and oven-roasting keep this dish much lighter. A quick marinara sauce with capers and green olives adds salty brininess. Creamy mozzarella, nutty parmesan, and fresh oregano finish it off beautifully (add basil leaves, if you wish).

Preheat the oven to 400°F (200°C).

Prepare the mushrooms: Tear the maitakes into medium pieces (about 1 inch/3 cm thick and 2 inches/5 cm long). Spread into an even layer on a large baking sheet. Drizzle the mushrooms with the oil and sprinkle with the salt and pepper. Toss the mushrooms with your hands to evenly coat them in oil, then top with panko and toss again. Spread them out in a single layer on the sheet (the panko will naturally nuzzle against the maitakes).

Roast for 20 to 25 minutes, flipping halfway through. The mushrooms should be soft and caramel-colored, but not crispy, and the panko should be a nice golden brown. Set aside to cool. Reduce the oven temperature to 350°F (177°C) and leave it on for baking the parm.

Meanwhile, make the sauce: Pour the tomatoes into a large bowl and crush with your hands, or use an immersion blender to get a smoother puree. (You might want to do this in the sink so you don't get spattered.)

In a large skillet, heat the oil over medium heat until it starts to shimmer. Add the garlic and cook until it just begins to brown on both sides. (Don't take your eyes off it, because garlic browns very quickly. You want it to be golden, not dark and bitter.) Remove from the heat and let the oil cool for a moment so that the tomatoes don't spatter you when you add them. Add the tomatoes and return to medium heat. Cook for about 10 minutes; if the tomatoes are particularly watery, let them reduce for an additional 10 minutes. Stir in the oregano, olives, and capers and set the sauce aside until ready to assemble the parm. Add the salt, taste, and add more if needed.

Assemble the parm: Spread a thin layer of sauce on the bottom of a 9 × 13-inch (23 × 33 cm) ceramic or glass baking dish. Add one-third of the mushrooms (and some toasted panko) in an even layer. Top with one-third of the remaining sauce and then one-third of the mozzarella slices. Sprinkle with one-third of the grated parmesan. Repeat the layering two more times, and finish by sprinkling the top with the oregano. Bake until bubbling and browned, about 45 minutes. Let cool for 15 minutes to set before serving.

COOKING WITH MUSHROOMS

MUSHROOMS, SAUSAGE, AND PEPPERS

SERVES 4

4 large Italian sausages (about
    4 oz/115 g each), scored in a
    few places
1 pound (455 g) fresh oyster
    mushrooms, trimmed and torn
1 pound (455 g) cherry tomatoes
    (I like them whole on the vine,
    but use whatever you can find)
2 bell peppers (red, yellow, or
    green), halved through the
    stem, with stems, ribs, and
    seeds removed
1 medium fennel bulb, halved
    through the root end, cored,
    and thinly sliced lengthwise
1 medium onion, 2 large shallots, or
    1 large leek, sliced in half
2 heads garlic, outer skin peeled
    off and tops trimmed slightly to
    expose the cloves
½ preserved lemon, store-bought
    or homemade (page 94), seeded
    and rind finely chopped
4 fresh oregano sprigs, leaves only
2 bay leaves
1 teaspoon fennel seeds
½ teaspoon Aleppo pepper
1 teaspoon flaky sea salt, such as
    Maldon
1 teaspoon cracked black pepper
¼ cup (60 ml) extra-virgin olive oil

This dish is inspired by my grandmother's sausage and peppers recipe. I use a sheet pan for convenience. This meal requires very little prep and is quite beautiful. I am working off a southern Italian flavor profile, with the sausage (salt-and-pepper or fennel), oregano, fennel, garlic, and lemon, but it's meant to be adaptable, so feel free to experiment with other ingredients, including mushrooms other than the oysters used here.

Position a rack in the center of the oven and preheat the oven to 425°F (220°C).

Dividing evenly, place the sausages on two sheet pans and arrange the mushrooms, tomatoes, bell peppers, and fresh fennel around them, taking care to not crowd the pan (you want everything to roast instead of steam). Add the onion, garlic, preserved lemon, oregano, bay leaves, fennel seeds, and Aleppo pepper. Finish with the salt, black pepper, and oil, tossing the ingredients to coat evenly.

Roast until the sausages are browned and cooked through and the peppers start to char on the edges, about 30 minutes.

Place the sausages on a serving platter, arrange the vegetables around them, and serve.

MUSHROOM RAGU

MAKES 3½ QUARTS (3.3 L)

8 tablespoons (4 oz/115 g)
  unsalted butter
4 tablespoons extra-virgin olive oil
3 celery stalks, finely chopped
2 medium carrots, finely chopped
1 yellow onion, finely chopped
1 large or 2 small leeks, thinly
  sliced and well washed
10 garlic cloves, smashed and
  peeled
¼ teaspoon Himalayan pink salt,
  plus more to taste
¼ teaspoon coarsely ground black
  pepper
2 tablespoons colatura di alici (or
  fish sauce, such as Red Boat)
2 pounds (910 g) mixed fresh
  mushrooms (such as maitake,
  shiitake, and oyster), trimmed
  and chopped extra fine
⅓ cup (30 g) porcini powder
1 cup (240 ml) dry white wine
2 cups (480 ml) mushroom broth,
  such as Everyday Mushroom
  Broth (page 80) or Lion's Mane
  Broth (page 82), or vegetable
  stock
Two 28-ounce (795 g) cans whole
  plum tomatoes, buzzed to a
  puree
1 cup (240 ml) heavy cream
1 cup (240 ml) whole milk
5 fresh oregano sprigs, leaves only
  (or 1 tablespoon dried oregano,
  preferably Sicilian)
2 tablespoons nutritional yeast
½ dried red chile, such as chile
  de árbol

Consider this mushroom recipe a project for a weekend or a lazy afternoon. It involves a fair amount of precise, repetitive chopping. You can chop the mushrooms in a food processor but do so in small batches and keep the chop a little rough. If you pulse them for too long, they will turn to paste. The goal is to chop the mushrooms to a texture that resembles ground meat. It shouldn't be minced, but should instead end up as smallish but irregular pieces. The result of all that chopping and the slow cooking is a delicious, deeply umami, Bolognese-style ragu. I like a combination of mushrooms in the ragu, for variety. I usually use maitake, shiitake, and oyster, to equal 2 pounds (910 g), but I've also made it with 2 pounds cremini mushrooms and it's perfectly delicious. Use whatever you prefer or can easily find, in whatever combination you like. The ragu tastes even better the second day. I suggest serving it over polenta or pasta, topped with finely grated pecorino or parmesan.

Preheat the oven to 250°F (120°C).

In a Dutch oven, heat 4 tablespoons of the butter and 2 tablespoons of the oil over low heat. When the butter has melted, make the soffritto (the vegetable base): add the celery, carrots, onion, leek, garlic, salt, and pepper and increase the heat to medium. Cook, stirring occasionally, until the onion is translucent but not browned, about 15 minutes (everything should be soft and mushy).

Add the colatura and the remaining 4 tablespoons butter and 2 tablespoons oil, stirring until incorporated. Add the chopped fresh mushrooms and mushroom powder and cook to allow the mushrooms to release moisture, 5 to 7 minutes, stirring occasionally. Add the wine and broth and cook until the sauce is reduced, about 5 minutes.

Add the pureed tomatoes, cream, milk, oregano, nutritional yeast, and chile. Simmer for 5 to 10 minutes, then cover and transfer to the oven. Cook until the ragu has reduced and deepened in color, stirring occasionally, about 3 hours.

Add salt to taste. If making ahead, let cool completely before transferring to glass jars or other storage containers. Refrigerate for up to 4 days or freeze for up to 4 months.

COOKING WITH MUSHROOMS

MUSHROOM LASAGNA

SERVES 6

1½ pounds (680 g) fresh
    mushrooms (I like a
    combination of oyster,
    chestnut, maitake, or beech)
6 tablespoons (3 oz/90 g)
    unsalted butter
6 garlic cloves, smashed and
    peeled
½ teaspoon Himalayan pink salt
Finely grated zest and juice of
    1 Meyer lemon
1 cup (240 ml) dry white wine
Cracked black pepper
2 cups (500 g) whole-milk ricotta
    cheese, preferably fresh
¾ cup (185 g) basil pesto
1 ball (8 to 10 oz/225 to 285 g) fresh
    mozzarella cheese, thinly sliced
1½ cups (150 g) finely grated
    pecorino cheese
1 cup (30 g) fresh basil leaves, plus
    more for topping
6 fresh lasagna sheets (6 ×
    8 inches/15 × 20 cm)
Fresh oregano sprigs
1 Meyer lemon, cut into wedges

This lasagna doesn't have any tomato, but it does have creamy ricotta mixed into a basil pesto with Meyer lemon and pungent oregano, and layers of woodsy, earthy chestnut mushrooms. If you happen to have any edible wild mushrooms on hand, this is a delicious place to use them. Black trumpets or chanterelles would be lovely here, as would wild or cultivated oyster mushrooms. It's such a crowd-pleaser, even mushroom skeptics will be coming back for more. It's worth seeking out fresh pasta sheets for this recipe or making your own; cut them to fit your pan as needed.

Preheat the oven to 350°F (177°C).

If using oyster or maitake mushrooms, tear them into small pieces. If using chestnut, trim and leave the stems on, and coarsely chop. If using beech mushrooms, trim and separate into strands.

In a heavy-bottomed medium pot, melt 3 tablespoons of the butter over medium heat. Add the mushrooms, garlic, and salt. Cook until softened, 3 to 5 minutes. Stir in the lemon zest and lemon juice. Add the remaining 3 tablespoons butter and the wine. Cook over medium heat until the liquid reduces and is saucy, the mushrooms are glossy (not watery), and the mixture is simmering, about 10 minutes. (Oyster mushrooms release more liquid, so the cooking time may vary.) Add a few turns of pepper. Remove from the heat.

In a medium bowl, combine the ricotta, pesto, and a few turns of pepper.

In a 9 × 13-inch (23 × 33 cm) baking dish, make layers in this order:

Layer 1: Add about one-quarter of the mushrooms and their cooking liquid to keep the first layer of pasta from sticking.

Layer 2: Add 2 lasagna sheets to fit in an even layer. Top with one-third of the ricotta mixture in 6 evenly spaced dollops. Add one-third of the remaining mushrooms, one-third of the mozzarella slices, one-third of the basil, and one-third of the grated pecorino.

Layers 3 and 4: Repeat layer 2, ending with the pecorino. Scatter a few oregano sprigs and basil leaves on top.

Bake until the top of the lasagna is browned and crispy, 25 to 35 minutes. Transfer to a rack to cool for 10 minutes before cutting.

Serve with Meyer lemon wedges, for squeezing.

COD POACHED IN PARCHMENT WITH ENOKI AND BEECH

SERVES 4

SAUCE
8 tablespoons (4 oz/115 g)
    unsalted butter
2 tablespoons yuzu juice
2 tablespoons ume plum vinegar
1 garlic clove, grated with a
    Microplane
1-inch (3 cm) nub fresh ginger,
    peeled and grated with a
    Microplane

PACKETS
1 large fennel bulb, halved
    through the root end,
    cored, and thinly sliced on a
    mandoline, plus the fronds
4 cod fillets (8 oz/225 g each)
½ teaspoon Himalayan pink salt
¼ cup (20 g) thinly sliced fresh
    lemongrass
¼ pound (115 g) enoki mushrooms,
    trimmed
¼ pound (115 g) brown beech
    mushrooms, trimmed

FOR GARNISH
Lemon wedges
Mixed fresh herbs, such as
    tarragon and parsley
Sliced scallions
Ume plum vinegar
Flaky sea salt, such as Maldon
Pickled ginger, turmeric, and fresh
    coriander seeds (optional)

It is so easy to cook in parchment once you get the hang of folding and sealing the paper. Here the fish and mushrooms gently poach in butter, lemongrass, yuzu juice, and ume plum vinegar. Make sure to take in all the gingery, garlicky, citrusy smells as you slit open the parchment at the table, and then top each serving with fresh herbs, sliced scallions, pickled fresh ginger, and perhaps a dash more ume plum vinegar. I use enoki and brown beech mushrooms for their delicate flavor, but you could substitute sliced cremini, small oyster mushrooms, or white beech. Baby shiitakes or small wild mushrooms like chanterelles would also work well.

Preheat the oven to 400°F (200°C).

Make the sauce: In a small saucepan, combine the butter, yuzu juice, vinegar, garlic, and ginger. Heat over low heat until the butter is melted and the flavors have melded.

Assemble the packets: Lay out four 13-inch (33 cm) squares of parchment paper on the counter. Fold each piece in half and crease, then unfold.

Dividing evenly, place the fennel slices on one half of each parchment square and top with a cod fillet. Sprinkle the pink salt evenly over the cod fillets. Scatter the lemongrass across each fillet and nestle the enoki and beech mushrooms against the sides of the fish. Spoon the sauce evenly over each fillet.

Fold the parchment over to enclose the ingredients, then form them into half-moon packets by pleating them: Beginning at one corner, make small overlapping pleats all the way around to tightly seal each. Transfer the packets to a sheet pan and roast for 20 minutes.

Carefully open the packets, taking care as the steam will be hot. Serve immediately with lemon wedges and other desired garnishes.

COOKING WITH MUSHROOMS

MUSHROOM BOURGUIGNON

SERVES 6

3 tablespoons all-purpose flour
½ teaspoon Himalayan pink salt,
   plus more to taste
½ teaspoon coarsely ground black
   pepper, plus more to taste
2 pounds (910 g) fresh cremini
   mushrooms, trimmed and
   halved (or quartered if large),
   or maitake, oyster, or chestnut
8 tablespoons (4 oz/115 g)
   unsalted butter
2 shallots, coarsely chopped
10 garlic cloves, smashed and
   peeled, plus 2 large heads
   garlic, halved horizontally
½ pound (225 g) pearl onions,
   trimmed
2 large carrots, cut into 1½-inch
   (4 cm) pieces, or 1 bunch small
   organic carrots, trimmed
2 cups (480 ml) red wine or orange
   wine with a little funk
2 teaspoons sherry vinegar
5 cups (1.25 L) mushroom broth,
   such as Everyday Mushroom
   Broth (page 80) or Lion's Mane
   Broth (page 82)
2 tablespoons colatura di alici (or
   fish sauce, such as Red Boat)
2 tablespoons tomato paste
½ cup (20 g) coarsely chopped
   fresh flat-leaf parsley, plus
   more for garnish
2 fresh bay leaves or 1 dried
Coarsely chopped fresh oregano
   leaves, for garnish (optional)

One of my favorite recipes to make during the colder months is bourguignon, a classic French dish I grew up eating on the heels of my stepmother's infatuation with Julia Child. These days, with so many vegetarians among our friends and family, and others who are looking to eat less meat, I adapted the classic beef stew to this mushroom version. The comforting, earthy dish is slow-cooked in the oven for a good 2 hours. I use colatura di alici here to add an underlying umami note. Homemade broth—either the Lion's Mane Broth (page 82) or Everyday Mushroom Broth (page 80)—gives the stew a more intense and layered mushroom flavor. Cremini is a classic choice for bourguignon, but it's also beautiful and delicious made with maitake, oyster, or chestnut mushrooms. Serve over buttery wide egg noodles, polenta, or potatoes (I like confit potatoes best with bourguignon).

Position a rack in the bottom third of the oven and preheat the oven to 300°F (150°C).

On a large sheet pan, toss the flour, salt, and pepper with your hands to combine. Dredge the mushrooms in the flour mixture.

In a heavy-bottomed ovenproof pot (I use a Dutch oven), heat 2 tablespoons of the butter over medium heat until melted. Cook about one-third of the dredged mushrooms in an even layer until browned on one side, 2 to 3 minutes. Flip and cook until browned on the other side, 1 to 2 minutes longer. With a slotted spoon, transfer the mushrooms to a plate and set aside. Repeat to brown the remaining mushrooms in two more batches, using 2 tablespoons butter for each.

Melt the remaining 2 tablespoons butter in the same pot. Add the shallots, smashed garlic, onions, and carrots and sauté until soft, about 3 minutes. Add the wine, vinegar, broth, colatura, tomato paste, parsley, bay leaves, and sautéed mushrooms to the pot. Bring to a simmer and cook for 5 minutes (just enough to bring everything together), then tuck the halved heads of garlic into the pot.

Transfer to the bottom rack of the oven and braise for 1 hour 30 minutes.

Before serving, remove and discard the garlic heads. Season the stew with more salt and pepper. Serve garnished with chopped parsley and oregano leaves (if using).

KING TRUMPET AU POIVRE

SERVES 4

4 or 5 large king trumpet (king oyster) mushrooms (about 1 lb/455 g total), with caps intact

7 tablespoons (3½ oz/100 g) cold unsalted butter

½ teaspoon Himalayan pink salt

4½ teaspoons cracked black pepper (use a mortar and pestle if you have one, or the loosest setting on a pepper grinder)

2 cups (480 ml) mushroom broth, such as Everyday Mushroom Broth (page 80) or Lion's Mane Broth (page 82)

⅓ cup (80 ml) dry white wine or Cognac

This recipe has serious steak frites vibes that remind me of early days in New York, when steak at midnight seemed like a good idea. I use a fragrant black pepper from Aranya, a gorgeous and lush hill station in the South of India that I visited a few years ago. I was so intrigued by the giant green cones of pepper hanging from trees that I smuggled some home and pickled them—but that's a story for another day. Thanks to our friends at Diaspora Co. (see the Source Guide, page 232), this gem of a pepper is now readily available in the US (no travel or smuggling needed!).

King trumpets are the perfect choice for the mushroom version of my beloved steak frites, which is cooked in the oven with mushroom broth and butter. The meaty, solid mushroom holds its shape under heat and becomes incredibly moist and juicy at the same time. It also takes well to the addictive au poivre sauce. Serve with crispy fries and a simple green salad.

Preheat the oven to 425°F (220°C).

Cut the mushrooms in half lengthwise, then score an "X" a few times down the rounded side of the stems.

Place the mushrooms cut side down in a 9 × 13-inch (23 × 33 cm) sheet pan (a quarter-sheet pan). Cut 4 tablespoons of the butter into ¼-inch (6 mm) cubes (16 total). Dot each mushroom with a couple of cubes of butter on the scored lines and sprinkle them all evenly with the salt and 2¼ teaspoons of the pepper. Pour 1½ cups (360 ml) of the mushroom broth into the pan so it pools around the mushrooms.

Roast for 40 minutes. Baste with the pan juices, then gently tip the sheet pan to pour the pan juices into a small saucepan.

Return the mushrooms to the oven and roast for about 10 minutes longer, until browned and the edges are just crispy (you want the insides to be a little soft).

Meanwhile, set the saucepan with the pan juices over low heat and add the remaining ½ cup (120 ml) broth, 3 tablespoons butter, and 2¼ teaspoons pepper. Heat until the butter is melted. Add the wine and increase the heat to medium, stirring constantly to incorporate. The sauce will thicken slightly as the alcohol evaporates. Reduce the heat to a simmer and cook until the sauce is thick enough to coat the back of a spoon, about 10 minutes.

Remove the mushrooms from the oven and transfer to a serving plate or platter. Spoon 1 tablespoon of sauce over each mushroom and serve immediately, with the remaining sauce on the side.

COOKING WITH MUSHROOMS

KING TRUMPET SCHNITZEL

SERVES 6

4 to 6 large king trumpet (king
    oyster) mushrooms (about
    1 lb/455 g)
4 cups (450 g) panko bread crumbs
½ teaspoon Himalayan pink salt
4½ teaspoons ground turmeric
6 large eggs
Coarsely ground black pepper
2 cups (480 ml) neutral oil, such
    as safflower, for frying
Flaky sea salt, such as Maldon,
    or Mushroom Salt (page 53),
    for finishing
1 Meyer lemon, cut into wedges,
    for serving
Mixed Herb Pesto (page 90),
    for serving
Green Cabbage Slaw with Citrus
    and Celery Seed (page 93),
    for serving

I love a schnitzel, a Milanese, a cutlet—call it what you will, but basically they are all fried pieces of heaven. Yes, I know they have subtle differences (duly noted for all you food academics out there). This mushroom version is destined to become a favorite if you are a fan of any fried cutlet. I slice large king trumpet mushrooms lengthwise into pieces. Each then gets gently pounded to tenderize or to split apart the fibrous interior and double-dipped in egg and salty turmeric panko. Finally, it's fried to a crispy golden brown. Serve with the herbaceous pesto and citrusy cabbage slaw.

Preheat the oven to 200°F (95°C).

Slice each mushroom lengthwise into 2 or 3 pieces, depending on the thickness. Using a mallet or rolling pin, gently pound the mushroom pieces, flattening the stems while taking care not to break them (they may split a bit, but they will hold together once you batter them).

Set up the ingredients for breading the mushrooms: In a wide shallow bowl, season 2 cups (225 g) of the panko with ¼ teaspoon of the pink salt and 2¼ teaspoons of the turmeric, tossing to combine. In a second wide shallow bowl, beat 3 of the eggs with a little pepper.

Working with one piece at a time, dip the mushroom slices in the eggs first, letting any excess drip off, then the panko, turning to coat completely. Set dipped pieces on a wire rack as you work.

Put the remaining 3 eggs in a clean wide shallow bowl and the remaining 2 cups (225 g) panko in another. Season the panko with the remaining ¼ teaspoon salt and 2¼ teaspoons turmeric. Beat the eggs with a little pepper. Dip the breaded mushroom slices again in the eggs, letting the excess drip off, and then the panko. Set the pieces aside until ready to fry.

In a deep cast-iron skillet or heavy-bottomed pan, heat the oil over medium heat until shimmering but not smoking, 340° to 350°F (170° to 177°C).

Working in batches, fry the breaded mushroom pieces until golden, 3 to 5 minutes per side, turning with a spider or tongs. If they brown too quickly, reduce the heat. Transfer to a sheet pan and keep warm in the oven until ready to serve.

Sprinkle with flaky salt. Serve with lemon wedges, pesto, and green cabbage slaw.

PORK CHOPS WITH MAITAKE AND PLUMS

SERVES 2

2 bone-in pork loin chops (about 1½ lb/680 g total)

Himalayan pink salt and coarsely ground black pepper

2 teaspoons maitake powder

1 tablespoon extra-virgin olive oil

1 tablespoon unsalted butter

1 shallot, finely chopped

½ pound (225 g) maitake mushrooms, trimmed and gently torn into medium pieces

18 sugar plums (about 1 lb/455 g), halved and pitted

A few fresh thyme and oregano sprigs

Sherry vinegar

In this twist on the classic pork chops and applesauce, the chops are pan-seared on the stovetop, roasted briefly in the oven to finish, and topped with plums and mushrooms. (I like the flavor of Berkshire heritage pork.) The soft, buttery texture of the maitakes merges with the jammy plums to create a sauce that's a little earthy, sweet, and sour all at once. I used small sugar plums, but you can swap in most any stone fruit, or even apples or seedless grapes. You can also substitute other mushrooms for the maitake; most will work well here.

Preheat the oven to 350°F (177°C).

Season the chops generously on both sides with salt and pepper and sprinkle evenly with the mushroom powder. In a large cast-iron skillet, heat the oil and butter over medium heat until shimmering. Add the chops and sear for 5 minutes per side, pressing down a little as they cook.

Transfer the skillet to the oven and roast the chops for 7 to 8 minutes.

Remove the chops and transfer to a plate. Tent with foil while you make the sauce.

Place the skillet over medium heat. Add the shallot, mushroom pieces, plums, herbs, and salt and pepper to taste and cook until soft and slightly jammy, 6 to 8 minutes. Finish with a splash or two of vinegar.

Serve the chops immediately, topped with the mushroom-plum sauce.

COOKING WITH MUSHROOMS

CRISPY RACK OF OYSTER MUSHROOM

SERVES 6

1 (3 to 4 lb/1.4 to 1.8 kg) fresh
    oyster mushroom (I use
    blue-gray)
Mixed fresh herbs, such as
    chives, thyme, mint, lovage,
    and marjoram (you want the
    equivalent of a largish farmers'
    market bunch, made up of a
    few different types)
3 heads garlic, 1 separated into
    cloves, smashed and peeled,
    and 2 left whole
1 large leek, cut into long strands
    and well washed
8 tablespoons ghee, melted
3 tablespoons Miso Mushroom
    Paste (page 57)
Himalayan pink salt and coarsely
    ground black pepper
1 Meyer lemon, halved
2 bay leaves

Have you ever seen one of those giant fans of oyster mushrooms at the farmers' market? You think, What is anyone going to do with a bunch of mushrooms that big? Fear not—I have you covered! First, buy one immediately. You want the freshest piece, ideally one about the size of a roasting chicken (3 to 4 pounds/1.4 to 1.8 kg).

A nice big oyster mushroom roasted whole is absolutely delicious, and can replace any big roast at the center of the table. The earthy, umami flavors of the versatile oyster mushroom are intensified by the generous slathering of ghee. If you don't have miso mushroom paste, just slather the mushroom with the melted ghee and dust it with miso powder or ground turmeric. You can also use lemon zest and juice with the ghee. The point is, this is a very forgiving recipe; use whatever seasonings you want, depending on what you plan to serve it with.

I like to serve the roasted mushroom with sautéed greens and roasted or smashed potatoes, or to chop it into small pieces with two knives and load them up in warm tortillas with Juniper-Pickled Onions (page 93) or radishes. This recipe is also multiseasonal. In spring I use ramps in place of the garlic and leek (and I season them with ramp salt), but green garlic, chives, garlic chives, and spring onion also work well in their place.

Preheat the oven to 375°F (190°C).

Place the mushroom in a large heavy-bottomed cast-iron skillet or roasting pan. Trim the herbs. If using whole sprigs, you don't have to remove the leaves from the stems. Tuck the peeled garlic cloves and herb sprigs deep inside the layers of the oyster mushroom, taking care to disperse them evenly. Tuck the leek strips in and around the mushroom, almost weaving them in. Spoon the melted ghee into a small bowl and combine with the miso mushroom paste until smooth. Using a spoon, scoop up a little bit of the ghee mixture at a time and pour into all the crevices of the mushroom, making sure to cover the top, bottom, and sides. Season all over with salt and pepper. Tuck the lemon halves, the whole heads of garlic, and the bay leaves into the pan, alongside the mushroom.

Cover the pan with foil and roast for 1 hour. Remove the foil, increase the oven temperature to 425°F (220°C), and roast until the mushroom is browned and crisp, about 10 minutes.

Let the mushroom rest for 10 minutes before transferring to a cutting board. Thinly slice and serve.

SALT AND PEPPER BRICK MUSHROOMS

SERVES 4

½ teaspoon Himalayan pink salt

½ teaspoon cracked black pepper

1 tablespoon extra-virgin olive oil

1½ pounds (680 g) fresh mushrooms, such as oyster, maitake, lion's mane, or portobello (one large piece or several medium pieces)

2 teaspoons capers, rinsed if salt-packed

1 lemon, cut into wedges, for serving

In this vegetarian riff on the classic brick chicken, mushrooms are simply cooked with a little olive oil, salt, and pepper, with capers added for zing. I have used oyster, maitake, and lion's mane—all are delicious. Each variety has a different moisture content and will release varying amounts of moisture as the mushrooms cook. I don't keep bricks in my kitchen, but a second cast-iron skillet or Dutch oven gets the job done. The weight of the second pan compresses the mushrooms and allows a nice crunchy crust to form while keeping them juicy and tender on the inside. Once you do this a couple of times, you might start keeping bricks in your kitchen!

In a small bowl, combine the salt and pepper.

In a large cast-iron skillet, heat the oil over medium-low heat until it begins to shimmer. Place the mushrooms in the skillet and sprinkle with half the salt and pepper mixture and half the capers. Cover the mushrooms with a sheet of foil, folding it into a round to cover the mushrooms and fit the contours of the skillet. Place a Dutch oven or another cast-iron skillet the same size as the first one on top of the foil. With two kitchen towels or oven mitts, press down firmly on the skillet to flatten the mushrooms beneath it; the mushrooms will release moisture as they cook. Press intermittently until a nice crust has formed, 10 to 12 minutes. Flip the mushrooms over, sprinkle with the remaining salt and pepper mixture and capers, and cook the other side the same way, weighting and pressing intermittently for about 10 minutes longer.

Remove from the heat and serve hot, with lemon wedges for squeezing.

DINNER FROM MUSHROOMS

BROTHY MUSHROOMS, BEANS, AND GREENS

SERVES 6 TO 8

1 cup (about 180 g) dried beans, such as flageolet, white, or navy

½ pound (225 g) fresh mushrooms (shiitake, maitake, oyster, or any type available)

½ cup (120 ml) plus 2 tablespoons extra-virgin olive oil, plus more for drizzling

1 head garlic, cloves separated, smashed, and peeled

1 large leek, thinly sliced and well washed

1 medium shallot, finely chopped

10 cups (2.4 L) mushroom broth, such as Everyday Mushroom Broth (page 80) or Lion's Mane Broth (page 82), or a combination of broth and water

1 parmesan or pecorino rind, plus grated cheese for serving

2 tablespoons Miso Mushroom Paste (page 57)

½ pound (230 g) agretti (2 large bunches) or other seasonal greens, trimmed and chopped

¼ dried red chile or ¼ teaspoon chile flakes (optional)

½ cup (25 g) fresh flat-leaf parsley leaves, coarsely chopped

¼ cup (7 g) fresh oregano leaves

½ cup (14 g) fresh mint leaves, coarsely chopped

1 teaspoon coriander seeds, crushed with the side of a knife

½ teaspoon coarsely ground black pepper, plus more for serving

1 teaspoon Himalayan pink salt, plus more to taste

1 lemon, halved, for serving

Chile flakes, for serving

Flaky sea salt, such as Maldon, for serving

I love to wander through the greenmarket without any particular recipe in mind, looking for what is in season and then forming ideas based on what I see. This recipe is adaptable enough to take you through all the seasons, depending on the greens and herbs that are available. It also freezes (and halves) easily. If I can find it, I include agretti (also called monk's beard), a delicate, salty, mineral-rich green from the samphire family. Otherwise, mustard greens, sorrel, young dandelion, escarole, spinach, radish greens, or radicchio all work well. I add a leek no matter what green I am using; the slow cooking brings out its sweetness. Use what inspires you, and if you have a question, ask the farmers for suggestions. More often than not, they are happy to chat. Serve with toasted Salty Sour Dark Rye (page 73) and Confit Mushrooms and Shallots (page 62), if desired.

In a large bowl, cover the beans with 2 quarts (2 L) water. Let them soak for at least 8 hours or up to overnight.

Preheat the oven to 300°F (150°C).

Gently shred or tear the maitake or oyster mushrooms into small pieces, or thinly slice the shiitakes.

In an 8- to 12-quart (7.6 to 11.3 L) heavy-bottomed ovenproof stockpot (or a large Dutch oven), heat ½ cup (120 ml) of the oil over medium heat until warm and shimmering. Add the garlic, leeks, shallot, and mushrooms. Cook until soft, about 5 minutes.

Drain the beans and add them to the pot along with the remaining 2 tablespoons oil, the mushroom broth, parmesan rind, miso mushroom paste, agretti, chile (if using), fresh herbs, coriander seeds, black pepper, and pink salt.

Cover, transfer to the oven, and braise for 3 hours.

Remove and discard the cheese rind. Ladle the broth and beans into bowls for serving. Finish each serving with pepper, grated cheese, a drizzle of oil, a squeeze of fresh lemon, chile flakes, and a pinch of flaky salt.

The brothy beans can be frozen for up to 3 months.

7

THE SWEETEST MUSHROOMS

COCONUT DARK CHOCOLATE PORCINI POTS DE CRÈME

SERVES 8

CUSTARD

1½ cups (360 ml) heavy cream, preferably organic

One 13.5-ounce (400 ml) can coconut cream

3 tablespoons porcini powder or Mushroom Powder for Sweets (page 50)

1 tablespoon chaga powder

¼ teaspoon Himalayan pink salt

8 ounces (225 g) bittersweet chocolate, finely chopped

6 large egg yolks, preferably organic

¼ cup (60 ml) maple syrup

Boiling water

FOR GARNISH

2 cups (480 ml) heavy cream, preferably organic

2 tablespoons maple syrup

1½ teaspoons porcini powder or Mushroom Powder for Sweets (page 50)

Flaky sea salt, such as Maldon

Chaga powder adds a floral note on the back end of this rich and delicious custard, while the earthy porcini dances with the dark chocolate and maple. Pot de crème is the kind of dessert I always ordered out until I realized how incredibly easy it is to make at home. Topped with maple whipped cream and a dusting of mushroom powder, it's an easy but impressive dessert for any holiday or special occasion.

Make the custard: Preheat the oven to 300°F (150°C).

In a small saucepan, whisk to combine the heavy cream, coconut cream, porcini powder, chaga powder, and pink salt. Bring to a simmer over medium-low heat (do not boil), then remove from the heat and cover the pot. Let the cream mixture infuse for 30 minutes.

Meanwhile, place the chopped chocolate in a heatproof bowl.

After 30 minutes, reheat the cream mixture over low heat. When it comes to a simmer, strain it through a fine-mesh sieve set over the bowl of chopped chocolate. Discard any mushroom pieces left in the sieve. Whisk to combine the chocolate and cream until smooth. Let cool until just warm (you don't want to cook the egg yolks when you add the chocolate).

In a large bowl, whisk the egg yolks and maple syrup until soft ribbons form, about 10 minutes by hand (my preferred method) or 4 to 5 minutes with an electric mixer on medium speed. Slowly fold the cooled chocolate cream by hand into the egg and maple mixture.

Divide evenly into eight 6-ounce (180 ml) ramekins.

Place the ramekins in a large, deep rectangular baking dish. Carefully fill the baking dish with boiling water to come halfway up the sides of the ramekins. Cover the dish with foil.

Bake until the edges and top of each have started to set, 25 to 35 minutes (check after 20 minutes). Transfer the baking dish to a wire rack. When the ramekins are cool enough to handle, transfer to the rack to cool.

Serve the pots de crème warm or chilled.

Make the garnish: Just before serving, whisk the heavy cream with the maple syrup in a bowl until soft peaks form. Garnish each pot de crème with a dollop of whipped cream, dust with the porcini powder, and sprinkle with flaky salt.

THE SWEETEST MUSHROOMS

COOKING WITH MUSHROOMS

MUSHROOM CHOCOLATE BARK

**MAKES ABOUT 2 POUNDS
(900 G)**

1 pound 8 ounces (680 g)
  bittersweet chocolate, finely
  chopped
2 tablespoons lion's mane powder
1 teaspoon flaky sea salt, such
  as Maldon, plus more for
  sprinkling
1 cup (150 g) mixed nuts, seeds, and
  dried fruit (I like golden raisins,
  blackberries, dried grapes on
  the stem, pistachios, walnuts,
  almonds, hazelnuts, candied
  ginger, dried hibiscus flowers,
  or dried organic rose petals)
⅓ cup (13 g) dried mushroom
  pieces, such as maitake, enoki,
  and lion's mane

If you are anything like me, you might find that your pantry is sometimes bursting with beautiful dried fruit and nuts. A perfect thing to do with this bounty is to make a chocolate bark. I've always been a fan of a nutty fruit bar, and this satisfies that craving. Recently, I started adding home-dried mushrooms (see How to Dry Mushrooms, page 38).

Consider making the bark around the holidays to share with friends or give as a gift, using whatever ingredients you have on hand. The recipe is meant to be fun and loose; you can even make it with an equal weight of chocolate chips, as I sometimes do. You will need a candy thermometer for tempering the chocolate, to avoid any "bloom" (white spots or streaks that appear on the surface of the chocolate due to fluctuations in temperature). Tempering creates a shiny hard chocolate that will snap when broken rather than bend or melt when touched. I make a thick bark in a large sheet pan; for a thinner bark, divide everything evenly between two smaller pans.

Line a large sheet pan with parchment paper.

Bring 1 inch (3 cm) of water to a simmer in a large deep saucepan over medium-low heat. In the meantime, place about two-thirds of the chocolate in a wide metal bowl. Place the bowl of chocolate over (not in) the saucepan (the bottom of the chocolate bowl should not touch the water) and turn off the heat. As the chocolate starts to melt, add the lion's mane powder and stir gently with a wooden spoon or flexible spatula until the chocolate reaches 110° to 115°F (43° to 46°C). Transfer the bowl to a tea towel and gradually stir in the remaining one-third of chocolate, a little at a time, letting it melt before adding more. Keep the thermometer in the chocolate. When it has reached about 82°F (28°C), return the water in the saucepan to a simmer, then turn off the heat and place the chocolate bowl back over it. Stir the chocolate until it reaches 88° to 90°F (31° to 32°C). Stir in the salt.

Test the chocolate by spreading a small spoonful onto the parchment with an offset spatula. Let it cool a bit. If properly tempered, it should look glossy, not dull or streaky. If not, repeat the process to get it to the right temperature.

Working quickly, carefully spread the chocolate evenly onto the sheet pan, about ½ inch (12 mm) thick. Gently sprinkle the nuts, seeds, fruit, and dried mushrooms over the warm chocolate so it sinks in just a little. Sprinkle evenly with salt.

Refrigerate the bark for 45 minutes to 1 hour to set. Once completely hardened, break or cut into desired pieces. The bark can be stored at room temperature for up to 1 week.

ANY FRUIT SEEDY SOY-MUSHROOM CRUMBLE

SERVES 6 TO 8

FILLING

6 cups (about 2 lb/910 g) fruit, one variety or a combination, such as sliced strawberries, peaches, apricots, plums, apples, pitted sour cherries, or blueberries

¼ cup (55 g) packed dark brown sugar

2 tablespoons yuzu juice or the juice of 1 lemon

TOPPING

1½ cups (170 g) almond flour

1 cup (90 g) gluten-free rolled oats, preferably organic

½ cup (15 g) red poha (flattened rice)

2 tablespoons sesame seeds

2 tablespoons raw, unsalted sunflower seeds

2 tablespoons pumpkin seeds

¼ cup (⅓ oz/10 g) dried lion's mane mushrooms, blitzed to a powder in a spice grinder, or 1 tablespoon lion's mane powder

¼ cup (⅓ oz/10 g) dried candy cap mushrooms, blitzed to a powder in a spice grinder, or 1 tablespoon candy cap powder

2 tablespoons dark soy sauce

½ cup (110 g) packed dark brown sugar

12 tablespoons (6 oz/170 g) cold unsalted butter, cut into tablespoons

Maple-sweetened whipped cream (see page 208) or Maple Mushroom Ice Cream (page 219), for serving

This dessert is easy to adapt to any fruit, in any season. The nutty, earthy saltiness of the crumble balances any sweet-tart fruit. I developed it for a friend who doesn't eat gluten. I was always baking a crostata or other desserts that she wasn't able to fully enjoy, since she was left to eat only the fruit and leave the crust behind. In place of flour, I added red poha, an Indian flattened rice, to bulk it up and add a little structure to the topping. You can find it at specialty grocers and online. Or just substitute the same amount of gluten-free oats in its place. Sour cherries, apricots, peaches, and apples pair beautifully with the buttery lion's mane and caramelly candy cap powders, but feel free to swap in porcini, maitake, or shiitake powders here.

Preheat the oven to 350°F (177°C).

Make the filling: In a large bowl, toss together the fruit, sugar, and yuzu juice. Let sit while you prepare the topping.

Make the topping: In another bowl, combine the almond flour, oats, poha, sesame seeds, sunflower seeds, pumpkin seeds, both mushroom powders, the soy sauce, and sugar. Add the cold butter. Using your fingertips or a pastry blender, combine the ingredients just until the butter is in small pieces and the mixture is crumbly (do not overmix).

Transfer the fruit to a deep ceramic or glass pie plate or a 9 × 13-inch (23 × 33 cm) baking dish. Scatter the topping evenly over the fruit. Bake until bubbling, 35 to 40 minutes.

Transfer to a wire rack to cool for 15 minutes or so, then serve warm with whipped cream or ice cream.

COOKING WITH MUSHROOMS

JUNIPER CHAGA PORCINI CRÈME CARAMEL

SERVES 6

15 juniper berries, crushed

1¼ cups (300 ml) heavy cream, preferably organic

1¼ cups (300 ml) whole milk, preferably organic

1 tablespoon chaga powder

2 tablespoons porcini powder

⅓ cup (80 ml) plus 2 tablespoons maple syrup

½ teaspoon Himalayan pink salt

7 stems (about 1¼ oz/35 g) fresh chamomile flowers (optional)

1 cup (200 g) organic cane sugar

2 tablespoons yuzu juice or juice of 1 lime

5 large eggs, preferably organic

Boiling water

Dried chamomile flowers, for garnish (optional)

Note: You will need a deep-dish pie plate or standard-size loaf pan or any other baking dish that holds at least 4 cups (1 L); I use a fluted, high-sided pudding mold.

This silky custard is a spin on a panna cotta I made with raw milk, juniper, and maple for a winter dinner with friends a few years ago. All the woodsy flavors—juniper, maple, chaga, and porcini—come into play here, reinforcing the idea that what grows together, goes together. The dark, bitter notes of the brown sugar caramel complement the earthiness of the mushrooms, while the citrus juice delivers welcome brightness and acidity (I like yuzu, but you can use lime in its place).

Finely chop 10 of the crushed juniper berries. In a saucepan, whisk together the chopped juniper berries, cream, milk, chaga powder, 1 tablespoon of the porcini powder, ⅓ cup (80 ml) of the maple syrup, and ¼ teaspoon of the salt. Bring to a gentle simmer over medium-low heat, then immediately turn it off. Do not let it come to a boil! Remove from the heat and add the fresh chamomile flowers, if using. Cover and set aside to infuse for 35 to 40 minutes.

Position a rack in the center of the oven and preheat the oven to 325°F (160°C). Place a baking dish (see Note) in the oven as it preheats (the heat will warm up the dish, helping to evenly distribute the caramel once you pour it in).

Strain the infused cream through an extra-fine mesh sieve. (If you don't have one fine enough, line it with cheesecloth.) You are straining out any particles of chaga, porcini, juniper, and chamomile. The chaga adds flavor to the cream, but the woody chaga remains undissolved; it has the texture of coffee grounds. Strain the cream twice if you think you need to remove any remaining bits (discard the chaga from the sieve).

In a heavy-bottomed saucepan, combine the sugar, yuzu juice, and the remaining 2 tablespoons maple syrup, 1 tablespoon porcini powder, ¼ teaspoon salt, and 5 crushed juniper berries. Cook over medium-low heat without stirring. The sugar will start to melt at the edges as it begins to caramelize. Stir in 3 tablespoons water. Increase the heat to medium-high and stir constantly until the sugar caramelizes, 2 to 3 minutes. It will take on a light amber color. The sugar will bubble up in the pot; stay attentive so it does not boil over. Boiling sugar is extremely hot. When the caramel is thick and golden amber in color, remove the warm baking dish from the oven and quickly pour the caramel into it, tilting it to cover the bottom. Set the dish aside. The caramel will harden and may make cracking noises as it cools, but don't worry, the caramel will liquefy again once it bakes and chills.

In a large bowl, whisk the eggs to combine. Set aside.

(continued)

Return the strained cream to the cleaned saucepan and heat over low heat until just warm, 2 to 3 minutes. Do not let it come to a boil! Remove from the heat and very gradually pour the warm cream into the beaten eggs, whisking slowly to allow the eggs to temper. Set the custard aside.

Place the baking dish with the caramel in the middle of a deep roasting pan. Pour the custard into the dish. Very carefully pour boiling water into the roasting pan to come about halfway up the sides of the dish, taking care not to let any water get into the custard.

Carefully transfer the roasting pan to the oven. Bake until the custard is set at the sides but still wobbly and soft in the center, 35 to 45 minutes, depending on the depth of your dish (start checking at 30 minutes). It will continue to set as it cools and even more as it chills.

Transfer the roasting pan to a wire rack and let the custard rest in the water bath for 15 to 20 minutes.

When the baking dish is cool enough to handle, cover it and refrigerate for at least 4 hours and up to a day or two ahead of serving. When you are ready to serve, slide a knife gently around the edges. Place a large plate over the crème caramel and flip it onto the plate. Pour any remaining caramel over the top. If desired, garnish with dried chamomile. Serve immediately.

COOKING WITH MUSHROOMS

MAPLE MUSHROOM ICE CREAM

SERVES 8 TO 10

¼ cup (10 g) Earthy Mushroom Powder (page 50)

¼ cup (5 g) dried candy cap mushrooms or other fragrant, earthy dried mushrooms, such as porcini

4 cups (1 L) heavy cream

2 cups (480 ml) whole milk

1 cup (240 ml) maple syrup

2 large pinches Celtic light grey sea salt

8 large egg yolks, preferably from super-happy chickens!

I love to make ice cream. It is so simple but feels so decadent, and the result is a bit of a love letter to whomever you are making it for. Good ingredients make all the difference, so if possible, use organic cream and milk and eggs with deep-yellow yolks. Flavorwise, this version goes almost to a salted caramel place. The top notes of porcini, maitake, and shiitake from the mushroom powder are wildly rich and earthy, while the candy cap adds a subtle umami-ness. The candy cap is the trickster of the mushroom world. It smells exactly like maple syrup but to me tastes nothing like maple, instead offering a deep floral, caramel note that brings out a rich sweetness when combined with maple. Grey sea salt adds just the right bit of minerality to the finish. Try a scoop with a shot of espresso poured over the top, for the most deeply delicious affogato.

In a heavy-bottomed saucepan, combine the mushroom powder, dried mushrooms, and cream and bring just to a simmer over medium heat. Remove from the heat, cover, and let steep for about 30 minutes. Do not let it boil. Strain the cream through a fine-mesh sieve into a bowl (discard any mushroom bits).

In another pot, combine the milk, ½ cup (120 ml) of the maple syrup, and the salt and bring to a gentle simmer over medium heat. Remove from the heat and set aside.

In a bowl, whisk the egg yolks with the remaining ½ cup (120 ml) maple syrup until they start to form a ribbon, 10 to 12 minutes by hand.

Gradually fold the warm milk mixture into the yolk mixture to temper the yolks.

Return the milk-yolk mixture to the saucepan and gently heat over medium-low heat, stirring constantly, until the mixture evenly coats the back of a wooden spoon, about 5 minutes. Do not let the custard boil!

Stir the infused cream gently into the custard until smooth. Refrigerate until it is good and cold all the way through, at least 2 hours.

Churn the mixture in an ice cream machine. If not serving immediately, transfer to an airtight container. The ice cream will keep in an airtight container in the freezer for up to 1 week.

SALTY MISO-MUSHROOM CARAMEL

MAKES 1½ CUPS (350 G)

1 cup (200 g) organic cane sugar

8 tablespoons (4 oz/115 g) cold unsalted butter, cut into cubes

1 tablespoon mushroom powder, any type (I like porcini, maitake, lion's mane, or candy cap), or Mushroom Powder for Sweets (page 50)

1 tablespoon Miso Mushroom Paste (page 57)

½ cup (120 ml) heavy cream

¼ teaspoon flaky sea salt, such as Maldon

My love for caramel is a holdover from childhood, when I was obsessed with Sugar Daddies and Sugar Babies (grainy, brown sugar caramel candies that came in little round pieces). To this day, I am much more of a caramel sundae person than a hot fudge, perhaps because I can taste the salt in caramel. This caramel is a little earthy, with notes of forest floor and wet leaves. It's the perfect accompaniment to the Maple Mushroom Ice Cream (page 219). You could also use it to make a chocolate, caramel, and sea salt tart, or anywhere you would use caramel. This is a dry caramel (sugar only) as opposed to a wet caramel, which uses a combination of sugar and water.

In a deep pot or saucepan, cook the sugar over medium-low heat, stirring constantly, until it starts to melt and liquefy, 8 to 10 minutes. Be careful, as it will get very hot. Remove from the heat.

Add the cubed butter, mushroom powder, and miso mushroom paste and stir or whisk to incorporate fully. Slowly stir in the cream until the mixture is smooth. Return to the stovetop and bring just to a boil over medium heat, watching the mixture closely to make sure it doesn't boil over (it will bubble up in the pan). When it rises in the pan, remove it from the heat.

Stir in the salt. Let the caramel cool completely, about 30 minutes.

Transfer to a glass jar. Cover and store in the refrigerator for up to 1 month. Reheat just before serving.

COOKING WITH MUSHROOMS

BROWN SUGAR BUTTERMILK PORCINI PUMPKIN PIE

MAKES ONE 9-INCH (23 CM) PIE

All-purpose flour, for dusting

½ recipe Pastry Dough (recipe follows)

One 15-ounce (425 g) can unsweetened pumpkin puree

1 vanilla bean, split lengthwise

⅔ cup (145 g) packed light brown sugar

½ teaspoon ground cinnamon

½ teaspoon freshly grated nutmeg

Seeds of 3 cardamom pods, crushed

2 tablespoons porcini powder, plus more for dusting

¼ teaspoon Himalayan pink salt

2 large eggs

1½ cups (360 ml) buttermilk

2 cups (480 ml) plus 2 tablespoons heavy cream

Demerara sugar or other coarse sugar, for sprinkling

2 tablespoons maple syrup

2 juniper berries, crushed with the side of a knife

This is a riff on my favorite of all varieties of pie, pumpkin. The porcini powder gives it an extra-earthy kick, while the buttermilk adds a nice tang. I love the grounding flavor that turmeric adds to the piecrust, but it is totally optional, so leave it out if you prefer.

On a lightly floured piece of parchment, roll the dough out into a 12-inch (30 cm) round. Lay the parchment over a 9-inch (23 cm) pie plate, centering the dough. Peel back the parchment and gently fit the dough into the pan. Crimp the edges and refrigerate the pie shell until firm, about 30 minutes.

Meanwhile, preheat the oven to 375°F (190°C).

Line the pie shell with parchment paper and fill with pie weights or dried beans. Transfer to the oven and bake until the crust is set, about 30 minutes. Remove the parchment and the pie weights and return the shell to the oven. Bake until the crust is light golden brown, about 10 minutes longer. Transfer to a wire rack while you make the filling.

Place the pumpkin puree in a bowl. Scrape the vanilla bean seeds into the pumpkin, then add the brown sugar, cinnamon, nutmeg, cardamom, porcini powder, salt, eggs, and buttermilk. Whisk everything together until just combined. Do not overmix or it will become too aerated!

Carefully pour the filling into the partially baked pie shell. Set on a sheet pan. Brush the crust with 2 tablespoons of the cream and sprinkle with demerara sugar.

Bake until the custard is set, about 1 hour (start checking at 45 to 50 minutes). Transfer to a wire rack to cool completely.

Whip the remaining 2 cups (480 ml) cream, maple syrup, and juniper berries until soft peaks form. Serve the pie at room temperature or chilled, with whipped cream and a dusting of porcini powder.

(continued)

Pastry Dough

MAKES ENOUGH FOR TWO
SINGLE-CRUST PIES

3½ cups (about 420 g) all-purpose
flour
1 teaspoon ground turmeric
(optional)
1 tablespoon organic cane sugar
½ teaspoon flaky sea salt, such
as Maldon
16 tablespoons (8 oz/284 g) cold
unsalted butter, cut into
1-tablespoon pieces
1 tablespoon apple cider vinegar
¼ cup (60 ml) ice water, plus more
if needed

*If you are making one single-crust pie, you can freeze the other half of
the dough for up to 6 months to use at a later date.*

In a large bowl, whisk together the flour, turmeric (if using), sugar, and
salt. Add the butter and vinegar and use your fingertips or a pastry
blender to mix the butter into the flour until the mixture resembles
coarse meal. (It's fine if some pieces of butter aren't fully incorporated;
this will make your pastry that much flakier.)

Add the ice water a little at a time as you form the pastry into a ball. It
should just hold together. If it doesn't hold together add a little more
ice water until it does.

Divide the dough in half and place each on a piece of parchment
paper. Flatten into discs and wrap in the paper. Chill until firm, 1 to
2 hours or overnight.

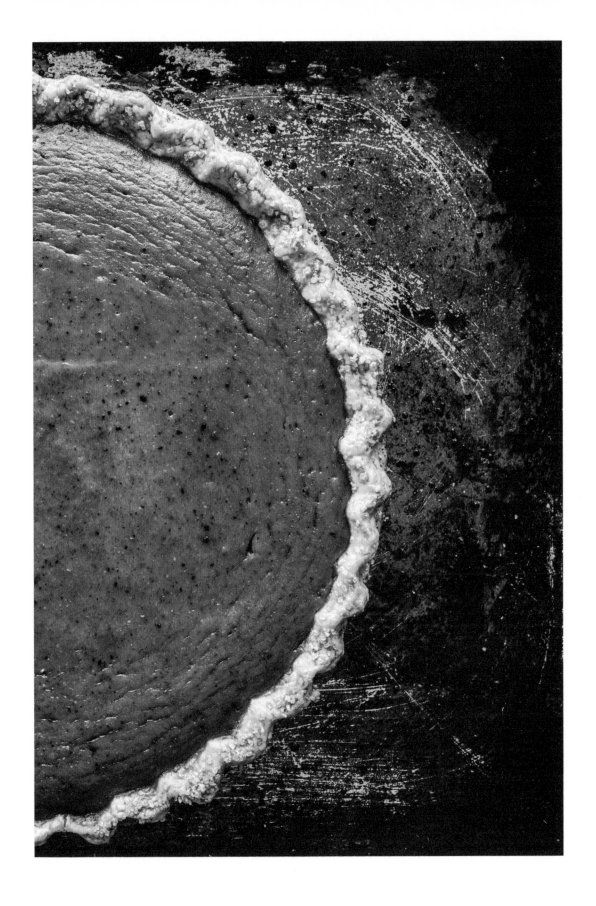

COOKING WITH MUSHROOMS

GINGER REISHI MAITAKE MOLASSES COOKIES

MAKES 36 COOKIES

DOUGH

12 tablespoons (6 oz/170 g)
    unsalted butter, at room
    temperature
¼ cup (75 g) organic molasses (not
    blackstrap; it is too bitter)
½ cup (70 g) jaggery powder
1 large egg, at room temperature
2½ cups (300 g) rye flour, plus
    more for shaping the dough
2 teaspoons baking soda
1 teaspoon freshly ground cloves
    (use a mortar and pestle or
    spice grinder)
1 teaspoon ground turmeric
1 teaspoon red reishi powder
1 teaspoon maitake powder
1 teaspoon lion's mane powder
½ teaspoon Himalayan pink salt
1-inch (3 cm) nub fresh ginger,
    peeled and finely grated
    with a Microplane (about
    1 tablespoon)

FOR TOPPING

1 piece (about 2 g) dried (cracker-
    dry) maitake mushroom, about
    the size of a plum
½ cup (105 g) demerara or organic
    cane sugar
Pinch of Himalayan pink salt

On a trip to visit the beautiful Ahilya Fort in India a few years ago, I tasted a ginger biscuit that immediately brought back the memory of my favorite childhood cookie, a soft ginger cookie, but it was spicier, with more depth. The difference was in the spices—cloves that had been freshly ground that morning and ginger that was freshly grated, not dried. The ratio of the spices was significantly higher than in the cookie I had grown up with, too. That memory inspired this cookie, which is also flavored with rye flour and a combination of mushroom powders—reishi, maitake, and lion's mane.

Make the dough: In a stand mixer with the paddle, beat the butter, molasses, and jaggery together until creamy. Add the egg and beat until just combined.

In a separate bowl, sift together the rye flour, baking soda, cloves, turmeric, all three mushroom powders, and the salt.

Slowly add the dry ingredients to the butter mixture, along with the ginger, beating on low until incorporated. The dough will be sticky. Scrape the sides of the bowl and the paddle with a flexible spatula.

Lightly flour your hands and form the dough into a disc. Wrap the dough in wax or parchment paper and refrigerate until firm, at least 1 hour and up to 24 hours. (The dough also freezes well.)

Meanwhile, make the topping: Crush the dried maitake mushroom over a small bowl (leaving some larger pieces about the size of tea leaves). Toss in the sugar and salt. Set aside.

Preheat the oven to 350°F (177°C).

Line two baking sheets with parchment paper. Unwrap the chilled dough. Using a tablespoon measure, scoop off a piece of dough and roll it into a ball. Dip the top side of the ball in the sugar dip and place sugar side up on the lined baking sheets. Repeat with remaining dough and sugar dip, arranging them about 3 inches (8 cm) apart. Sprinkle each ball with 2 to 3 drops of water and some salt.

Bake until the cookies are set but not hard, 6 to 8 minutes. They will seem very soft when you remove them from the oven. Let them cool on the sheet for a minute or two before transferring to a wire rack to cool. Let cool completely and devour.

The cookies keep well in an airtight container for up to 1 week.

'SHROOMY NUT BUTTER CHOCOLATE CHUNK COOKIES

MAKES 20 COOKIES

Olive-oil cooking spray for the pan

2 cups (455g) 'Shroomy Nut and Seed Butter (page 61; made without the optional maple syrup)

1½ teaspoons Miso Mushroom Paste (page 57)

2 large eggs

1 cup (200 g) packed brown sugar or 1 cup (145 g) date sugar

3 tablespoons shiitake powder

¼ teaspoon flaky sea salt, such as Maldon, plus more for sprinkling

6 ounces (170 g) dark chocolate (70% cacao) chunks, coarsely chopped, or bittersweet chocolate chips

This woodsy, gluten-free take on a traditional peanut butter cookie is chock-full of deep flavor, thanks to the miso mushroom paste, 'shroomy nut butter, and big chunks of dark chocolate. Resist the temptation to swap in another nut butter for the 'shroomy nut butter. Not all blends are created equal, and the differences in fat and oil content react differently while baking. Brown sugar delivers a slight caramel note without being too sweet. Instead, the cookies are nutty, earthy, a little salty, and chocolaty. What else could you ask for in a cookie?

Preheat the oven to 350°F (177°C). Lightly mist two baking sheets with cooking spray.

In a medium bowl, stir to combine the nut butter, miso mushroom paste, eggs, sugar, shiitake powder, and salt. Fold in the chocolate. Refrigerate the dough until firm, about 30 minutes.

Using a medium (2-tablespoon) ice cream scoop, arrange balls of dough on the prepared sheets about 2 inches (5 cm) apart (they don't spread out while they bake). Flatten slightly with the palm of your hand or the bottom of a measuring cup, and sprinkle lightly with salt.

Bake until the cookies are set on the outside and browned on the bottom (the insides will still be soft), 10 to 12 minutes. Transfer the sheets to a wire rack. Let the cookies cool for 5 minutes on the sheets before transferring to a wire rack to cool completely.

The cookies should keep in an airtight container at room temperature for up to 4 days.

DOUBLE-CHOCOLATE TAHINI MUSHROOM BROWNIES

MAKES 9 BROWNIES

Softened butter and unsweetened
   cocoa powder for the pan
12 tablespoons (6 oz/170 g)
   unsalted butter, cut into pieces
8 ounces (225 g) bittersweet
   dark chocolate (70% cacao),
   chopped into small pieces
¼ cup (60 g) tahini, preferably
   organic (I use Seed and Mill
   brand)
1 tablespoon candy cap powder
1 tablespoon lion's mane powder
½ teaspoon Himalayan pink salt
3 large eggs, preferably organic,
   at room temperature
1½ cups (350 g) packed light
   brown sugar
½ cup (60 g) all-purpose flour
¼ cup (35 g) rye flour
¼ cup (40 g) semisweet chocolate
   chips
1 tablespoon black sesame seeds
¼ teaspoon flaky sea salt, such as
   Maldon, plus more for topping
Mushroom powder of your choice,
   for topping (optional)

I am not a sweets person, generally, and usually temper any sweet I eat with a fair amount of savory ingredients, so including mushrooms and tahini here makes a lot of sense. Candy cap mushroom powder brings in a floral note and maple aroma, while the lion's mane adds a buttery earthiness. Feel free to swap the lion's mane for another earthy mushroom, such as porcini, shiitake, or maitake, or the Mushroom Powder for Sweets (page 50). Just before baking, top with sesame seeds and sea salt. Dust with mushroom powder or dark cocoa powder and more sea salt before serving. If you are feeling adventurous, serve each brownie with a giant scoop of Maple Mushroom Ice Cream (page 219).

Preheat the oven to 350°F (177°C). Brush a 9-inch (23 cm) square baking pan with softened butter and dust with cocoa powder.

In a medium saucepan, combine the butter, chocolate, tahini, mushroom powders, and pink salt. Heat over low heat until the butter and chocolate are melted and smooth, whisking to incorporate all the ingredients. Remove the pan from the heat and set aside to cool for 5 minutes.

Meanwhile, in a medium bowl, whisk the eggs. Add the sugar and whisk by hand until fully incorporated and starting to ribbon, about 10 minutes. The eggs and sugar almost double in size when they have ribboned and have a light caramel color. It should ribbon off the back of the whisk. (I prefer to do this by hand, which takes a lot of arm strength, but you can use an electric mixer if you prefer; it should take about 5 minutes.)

Slowly fold the cooled chocolate mixture into the egg mixture with a flexible spatula.

In a small bowl, whisk together the all-purpose and rye flours. In two batches, fold the flour mixture into the chocolate mixture until just combined and no streaks remain. Fold in the chocolate chips. Transfer the batter to the prepared pan and smooth the top. Sprinkle with the sesame seeds and flaky salt.

Bake until a skewer inserted in the center comes out clean, about 35 minutes (check after 30 minutes).

Transfer the pan to a wire rack. Let the brownies cool completely in the pan. Once the brownies have cooled, dust with mushroom powder, if you like, and flaky salt. The brownies should keep for up to 1 week, well wrapped, at room temperature.

SOURCE GUIDE

Bulich Mushrooms
ourharvest.com/suppliers/
bulich-mushroom-farm
Catskills, New York

Burlap & Barrel
burlapandbarrel.com
Single-origin spices and herbs
IG: @burlapandbarrel

**Connie Green at Wine Forest
Wild Foods**
wineforest.com
Purveyors of wild mushrooms
and foods
Napa, California
IG: @conniegreenwineforest

Dan Madura Junior Farm
johndmadurafarms.com
Exotic cultivated mushrooms
Orange County, New York

Diaspora Co.
diasporaco.com
Single-origin spices, seeds, chiles,
and dried herbs and flowers
Oakland, California
IG: @diasporaco

Duals Natural
dualsnatural.com
Spices, herbs, and specialty foods
New York, New York

Dunks Mushrooms
dunksmushrooms.com
William J. Dunkerley
Brentwood, New Hampshire
IG: @dunksmushrooms

Farmer Ground Flour
farmergroundflour.com
Organic flours and grains
from New York State
Trumansburg, New York
IG: @farmergroundflour

Far West Fungi
farwestfungi.com
San Francisco, California
IG: @farwestfungi

Fresh Catskills
freshcatskills.com
Upstate New York
Laura@freshcatskills
IG: @freshcatskills

Gail's Farm
localhens.com/farms/gails-farm
New Jersey

Henry Street Studio
henrystreetstudio.com
Handmade ceramics
Chatham, New York
IG: @henrystreetstudio

Herban Cura
herbancura.com
Herbal tinctures, salves,
teas, and oils
New York, New York
IG: @herban.cura

Janaki Larsen Studio
janakilarsenceramics.com
Handmade ceramics
Vancouver, British Columbia
IG: @janakilarsen

Kalustyan's
Kalustyans.com
Spices, dried and powdered
mushrooms, and specialty
ingredients
IG: @kalustyans

Les Hook and Nova Lee
thevermonters.com
Wildcrafters and educators

Lucky Dog
luckydogorganic.com
Hamden, New York
IG: @luckydogorganic

Meadows and More
meadowsandmore.com
Wildcrafter and author
New Jersey
IG: @meadowsandmore

Mushroom Spirits Distillery
mushroomspiritsdistillery.com
Seneca Falls, New York
IG: @mushroomspirits

Natoora
natoora.com
Specialty produce, pantry items,
and wild foods
IG: @natoora

North Spore
northspore.com
Mushroom spawn and growing kits
IG: @northsporemushrooms

Peace and Plenty Farm
peaceplentyfarm.com
American-grown saffron
Kelseyville, California
IG: @peaceandplentyfarmer

Regalis Foods
regalisfoods.com/collections/
wild-edibles
Wild and cultivated mushrooms,
specialty produce, pantry items,
and wild foods
New York, New York
IG: @regalisfoods

Riot Rye
riotrye.ie
Bakehouse and bread school
Tipperary, Ireland
IG: @riotrye_

RW Guild
rwguild.com
Ceramics, glass, and textiles
New York, New York
IG: @rwguild

Smallhold
smallhold.com
Fresh mushrooms and mushroom
growing kits
New York City area
IG: @smallhold

Smugtown Mushrooms
smugtownmushrooms.com
Dried mushrooms and extracts,
and grow kits
Rochester, New York
IG: @smugtownmushrooms

SOS Chefs
sos-chefs.com
Fresh and dried mushrooms,
miso powder, spices, and unique
pantry ingredients
East Village, New York City
IG: @soschefs

Sun Potion
sunpotion.com
Powdered mushrooms, herbs and
adaptogens, and ashwagandha
IG: @sunpotion

Tivoli Mushrooms
tivolimushrooms.com
Cultivated and wild mushrooms
from the Catskills and beyond
Hudson, New York
IG: @tivolimushrooms

Wurtz Ceramics
khwurtz.dk
Handmade ceramics
Denmark
IG: @wirtzaage

RECOMMENDED READING

Arora, David. *Mushrooms Demystified*

Bray, Richard. *Healing Mushrooms: A Practical Guide to Medicinal Mushrooms*

Cage, John. *A Mycological Foray*

Cotter, Tradd. *Organic Mushroom Farming and Mycoremediation*

Hobbs, Christopher. *Medicinal Mushrooms: The Essential Guide*

Isokauppila, Tero. *Healing Mushrooms: A Practical and Culinary Guide to Using Mushrooms for Whole Body Health*

Rogers, Robert. *Medicinal Mushrooms: The Human Clinical Trials*

——. *Mushroom Essences: Vibrational Healing from the Kingdom Fungi*

Stamets, Paul. *Growing Gourmet and Medicinal Mushrooms*

ACKNOWLEDGMENTS

As they say, it takes a village, and this book was no exception. A special thank-you to my editor, Lia Ronnen, for igniting this project, and the incredible team at Artisan: Suet Chong, Zach Greenwald, Nancy Murray, Bella Lemos, Jane Treuhaft, and Allison McGeehon. Thank you to Katherine Cowles, my book agent, for pushing me to grab hold of my ideas and never giving up on me all these years. To Lucia Bell Epstein, who was there at the inception of this project and stayed the course, working many long days, testing, writing, cooking, shopping, note taking, and keeping it all calm. I could not have done it without you. To Ellen Morrissey, for the many hours of work it took to realize this project. I so appreciate the wisdom, guidance, and knowledge that came with your help. To Frances Boswell and Ayesha Patel for many years of friendship and for bringing the magic and style. To my core team: Sarah Laird, Joyce Mills, Biddy Marquis, Lee Anne Grove, Francesca Crichton, Sahara Ndiaye, Anna Sophia John, and Madeleine Peacock.

To Aran Goyoaga, Heidi Swanson, and Deborah Williamson for their friendship and guidance. To Amy Chaplin, Sara Copeland, Carla Lalli Music, Elissa Altman, Fanny Singer, Susan Spungen, Tamar Adler, and Cliodnah Prendergast for friendship and inspiration.

Thank you to Nancy Jo Iacoi for always listening to new ideas and being my market cohort. To Susan Barber for her wisdom and beautiful design.

To the many hands that assisted in the kitchen: Imogen Kwok, Sadie Hope-Gund, Nhumi Threadgill, and Denise Ginley.

To my friends at Smallhold, Tivoli Mushrooms, North Spore, and Smugtown Mushrooms for their advice, guidance, and generosity with mushrooms and knowledge.

Thank you to all the people who have shared a meal and taste-tested the recipes: Cameron Carter, Nayli Gilbertsen, Ana Marino, Grace Milk, Amira Chandani, Sophia Pappas, Susan Bell and Mitch Epstien. To the Barn crew; India D'Arthenay Adams, Luke Meyer, Odette Esme Meyer Adams, Eden James Meyer Adams, Otto Meyer Adams, Nate Smith, Sophie Kamin, Ever Smith, Bay Smith, Paola Ambrosi Di Magistris, Murray Hall, Hedi Gaia Hall, Gurumaan Khalsa, Gemma Corsano, Andy Ingalls, Alicia Abuliak, Pablo Abuliak, Enzo Abuliak, Blue Abuliak, Electra Abuliak, and Vida Ehn.

To Dana Gallagher and Imogen Miller for housing us, offering advice, and sharing many mushroom meals. To Les and Nova for showing me the way to the forest and to Evan Strusinski for the back-of-the-trunk deliveries. Thank you to my husband, Martin Hyers, for all the mushroom pickups, no matter how far, and to Lula and Sam for their humor and unconditional love. I promise I will cook something other than mushrooms soon.

INDEX

ANDREA GENTL IS
AN AWARD-WINNING
FOOD AND TRAVEL
PHOTOGRAPHER. OVER
THE SPAN OF HER
30-YEAR CAREER, SHE
HAS PHOTOGRAPHED THE
WORLD'S LEADING CHEFS
AND CULINARY PIONEERS
WHILE TELLING A DISTINCT
STORY, ENTIRELY HER
OWN, THROUGH HER
IMAGES. IT IS FROM THAT
PERSPECTIVE, AS WELL
AS THROUGH EXTENSIVE
GLOBAL TRAVEL, THAT
SHE WRITES, COOKS, AND
CREATES. GENTL WORKS
IN COLLABORATION
WITH HER HUSBAND AND
PARTNER, MARTIN HYERS.